LE NAVET BETE

Le Navet Bete is a physical-comedy theatre company based in Exeter, Devon, whose spectacular and hilarious shows have wowed audiences globally since their formation in 2007. The company of five (Al Dunn, Matt Freeman, Dan Bianchi, Nick Bunt and Alex Best) first met each other whilst studying on the Theatre and Performance course at the University of Plymouth in 2003 and, since graduating, have produced twelve indoor and three outdoor performances to huge critical acclaim and success. Their first two shows *Serendipity* and *Zemblanity*, heavily influenced by *bouffon* and non-narrative-based structures, were performed at the Edinburgh Festival Fringe in 2008 and 2009 respectively and gained multiple five-star reviews. As the company developed and grew over the following years, their inimitable style of performance became much more storytelling/narrative-driven with hit shows such as *The Wonderful Wizard of Oz*, *Dick Tracy* and *Robin Hood and His Merry Men* placing physical theatre, fooling and slapstick at the heart of it. With Exeter as their base, they are Associate Artists at the Exeter Northcott Theatre, where *Dracula: The Bloody Truth* premiered in 2017. The company are also Artists in Residence at the Exeter Phoenix and are co-producing partners with the Barbican Theatre, Plymouth, to deliver their annual Christmas show to sell-out audiences every year. Making accessible work has been at the centre of Le Navet Bete's ethos right from the very beginning. This saw them diversify into outdoor performance in 2010, quickly becoming one of the UK's most ridiculously outrageous, much-loved outdoor acts. They have since performed thousands of outdoor shows from the circus fields at Glastonbury Festival, and the beautiful gardens of the Herrenhausen Palace in Hanover, Germany, to the picturesque *Plaza de Armas* in Morelia, Mexico, and high up on the side of the Rock of Gibraltar. As well as performing, the company have a widely renowned education programme specialising in clowning, physical comedy, performer–audience relationships and play, that they have taught in schools, colleges and universities across the world from the Royal Central School of Speech and Drama in London to the Universidad Nacional Autónoma de México in Mexico City. *Dracula: The Bloody Truth* is Le Navet Bete's third collaboration with John Nicholson at the directing helm. Their partnership has flourished since working together in 2013 on *Once Upon a Time in a Western*, allowing creativity and comedy to collide and leading to their best work to date.

JOHN NICHOLSON

John Nicholson is a writer, performer and director and an Artistic Director of the award-winning Peepolykus, with whom he has created twelve productions that have toured the company worldwide, and into the West End with *The Hound of the Baskervilles* (West Yorkshire Playhouse). This comic adaptation, co-written with Steven Canny, has been licensed all over the world, with fifty or so US productions to date. This, alongside *The Massive Tragedy of Madame Bovary* (co-written with Javier Marzan) is published by Nick Hern Books. Further writing/directing credits include *Shaun the Sheep* (Aardman); *No Wise Men* (Liverpool Playhouse, Bristol Old Vic); *Dick Tracy* (Le Navet Bete); *Paul Merton – My Obsession* (Edinburgh); *Spyski – The Importance of Being Honest* (Lyric Hammersmith); *The Arthur Conan Doyle Appreciation Society* (Traverse, Edinburgh); *Richard III's Rampage* for the Kevin Spacey Foundation (world tour); Nina Conti in *Dolly Mixtures* (Sydney Opera House, West End); *Help! My Life is a Musical* for NYMT:UK (winner of MTM Award); Mike McShane in *Mon Droit* (Edinburgh Festival); *Paul Merton – Out of His Head* (Vaudeville, West End); *Origins* (Pentabus); *Spymonkey's Spookshow* (Blackpool Winter Gardens); *A Little Hotel on the Side* (Bath Theatre Royal); *Marley was Dead, Baskervilles, A Trespasser's Guide to the Classics* – series 1 and 2, *Rik Mayall's Bedside Tales* (BBC Radio 4); *Under Surveillance, Comedy Nation* (BBC 3); *A Salted Nut* (Paramount); *The Mulligans, Off Their Rockers* (ITV). John has recently written a bespoke improvisation course for teachers (under the auspices of King's College, London). For further information, please visit peepolykus.com.

Le Navet Bete & John Nicholson

DRACULA:
THE BLOODY TRUTH

NICK HERN BOOKS

London

www.nickhernbooks.co.uk

A Nick Hern Book

Dracula: The Bloody Truth first published in Great Britain in 2017 as a paperback original by Nick Hern Books Limited, The Glasshouse, 49a Goldhawk Road, London W12 8QP, in association with Le Navet Bete

Dracula: The Bloody Truth copyright © 2017 Le Navet Bete and John Nicholson

Le Navet Bete and John Nicholson have asserted their moral right to be identified as the authors of this work

Cover photograph by Matt Austin

Designed and typeset by Nick Hern Books, London
Printed in the UK by Mimeo Ltd, Huntingdon, Cambridgeshire PE29 6XX

A CIP catalogue record for this book is available from the British Library

ISBN 978 1 84842 703 7

A Note from the Authors

The script you're holding evolved through a process of devising in response to writing, and then writing in response to devising, and then writing in response to rehearsal. Although we wanted to make a comedy, we didn't want to write a comedy. Or rather, we wanted to write a play about Dracula that was extremely loyal to Bram Stoker's original story. The comedy, we decided, would emerge from the framing device – the idea that Van Helsing, who hates theatre, has hired three idiots to help him broadcast the true events that happened to him and his friends; the true events that Stoker has shamelessly fictionalised.

So in this respect, this play is not a spoof version of *Dracula*. It's a serious (albeit wooden) script, within which terrible directorial decisions have been made and which is primed to derail at every turn. But despite all, the company somehow pull it off. One of the delights of the production is the sheer number of quick-changes the cast of four have to accomplish in order to play the forty or so characters. Sometimes the actors share characters, sometimes an actor is keeping three characters alive in one scene. As in a breakneck farce, the timing must be nanosecond precise in order to nail the comedy. The most commonly used word in rehearsal was: 'Again!'

This play is the result of the collaboration from the whole creative team – from initial planning meetings through to the end of rehearsals. Aside from the brilliant and joyful Le Navet Bete company (Al Dunn, Matt Freeman, Dan Bianchi, Nick Bunt and Alex Best), credit must go to Phil Eddolls for his ingenious set design, Peter Coyte for his inspirational composition, and Sarah Dicks for her superbly realised costumes, all of which influenced the direction of the writing.

If you are keen to perform this play, we'd love to chat. It's worth bearing in mind a few things. Firstly, although it was written for Le Navet Bete, a company who happen to be made up of four male performers, the play would work just as well if the cast was of mixed gender. The most obvious opportunity would be for Matt's part to be played by a woman. Also, although part of the fun is the challenge of all the quick-changes, additional cast members could be brought in and the characters shared further.

Another discussion point will be the set, or rather, the three sets! The framing device is that the play is taking place in 1900, so we began with the idea of a set (or set elements) that help the audience suspend their disbelief in that respect. On top of this, Van Helsing has gathered furniture from around his house to help recreate various locations. When the company accidentally destroy the back wall at the end of the first half, they discover a rather hammy, French-brace-style set which is much more theatrical than Van Helsing's furniture. So that gets incorporated into their retelling. In the original production, this concept was fully realised. But it could easily be simplified for other mountings of this script. A film of the original show is available from info@lenavetbete.com.

Happy reading!

John Nicholson

To those of you are about to delve into these pages, we hope you have as much fun reading/performing it as we did! Finally, we would like to thank our incredibly loyal fans and audiences who have continued to support our work over the past ten years. You are why we do what we do. That shared joy, fun, excitement and anticipation in the theatre is electric; something very special. Long may this continue.

LNB x

Dracula: The Bloody Truth was first performed by Le Navet Bete at the Exeter Northcott Theatre on 30 March 2017. The cast was as follows:

ACTOR 1	Nick Bunt
ACTOR 2	Dan Bianchi
ACTOR 3	Matt Freeman
ACTOR 4	Al Dunn

Director	John Nicholson
Production & Technical Manager	Alex Best
Set Designer	Phil Eddolls
Set Builders	Belgrade Theatre Production Services
Costume Designer	Sarah Dicks
Composer/Sound Designer	Peter Coyte
Lighting Designer	Marcus Bartlett
Choreographer	Lula Nicholson
Scenic Artist	Nina Raines
Magic Consultant	John Bulleid
Stage Manager	Abi Cowan
Carpenter	Spencer Rouse
Wardrobe Assistant	Georgia Burgess
Graphic Designer	Dave Robertson
Artistic Photographer	Matt Austin
Production Photographer	Mark Dawson
Show Trailer Videographer	Simon Burbage

DRACULA: THE BLOODY TRUTH

Le Navet Bete & John Nicholson

2

Characters

ACTOR 1, *Nick*
ACTOR 2, *Dan*
ACTOR 3, *Matt*
ACTOR 4, *Al*
MAN IN DJ
PROFESSOR VAN HELSING
JONATHAN HARKER
CART DRIVER
CART DRIVER'S WIFE
DRACULA
BRIDE 1
BRIDE 2
BRIDE 3
PEASANT
MINA MURRAY
TRAIN CONDUCTOR
LUCY WESTENRA
MRS WESTENRA
DR SEWARD
QUINCEY MORRIS
HOLMWOOD
DOCK WORKER
SHIP'S CAPTAIN
SHIP'S FIRST MATE
DAD *and* SON ON CLIFF
BLOKE
BOX MAN
MARGARET
RENFIELD
PAPERBOY
DOCK BOY

Note on Play

The play is written for four actors who play forty characters. The actors play versions of themselves when they talk directly to the audience, or when they're 'outside of the play'. On these occasions, the names of the original actors are used in this script. But, as with place names and the name of the audience member, please adjust accordingly if you are performing this script.

The advised casting works as follows:

ACTOR 1 (*Nick*), Professor Van Helsing, Bride 1, Quincey Morris, Peasant, Train Conductor, Bloke, Box Man, Paper Boy

ACTOR 2 (*Dan*), Dracula, Dr Seward, Bride 3, Dad and Son on Cliff, Mrs Westenra, Cart Driver

ACTOR 3 (*Matt*), Man in DJ, Mina Murray, Holmwood, Dock Worker, Bride 2, Mrs Westenra, Ship's First Mate, Cart Driver's Wife, Margaret

ACTOR 4 (*Al*), Jonathan Harker, Lucy Westenra, Renfield, Ship's Captain, Cart Driver's Wife, Dock Boy

The set creates a proscenium arch with curtains and a 'brick' theatre back wall with a locked door. There are doors on either side of the pros. The intention is to give the impression that we are in a Victorian theatre.

In Act One, the set consists of Van Helsing's furniture – a screen (with three doors cut into it), a cart (that doubles as a table), a wardrobe, a couple of tables and chairs, and a few tea chests.

In Act Two, the company bring on a new set they discovered behind the back wall. It consists of three painted stage flats, with a door in one.

ACT ONE

Scene One

Downstage in front of the curtains a gramophone is playing. The curtains open to reveal a MAN IN A DJ *sat behind a table set for supper. He removes the lid from the platter and serves himself some food. He pours himself a glass of wine. The lights flicker. As he reaches for the glass it mysteriously drains. The needle suddenly pulls across the record.*

Salt and pepper pots slide across the table. A book flips open. A photo rises out of another. The man stands and his wig flies off. His head appears to fall off his shoulders. A fork flies off the table. He sits, clutching his heart.

An arm bursts through his plate and grabs his neck. The hand grabs his tongue and stretches it. The man is pulled face down onto his plate. He lurches back. The food on the platter shakes. The man brings the lid down on it but is then thrown backwards and so, lifting the lid, he reveals VAN HELSING*'s head on the platter.*

VAN HELSING. Are you scared? Of course you're not.

The salt and pepper pots move around the platter.

Scene Two

AL *enters through downstage-right door while* VAN HELSING *extracts himself from beneath the table in semi-light.*

AL. People of Exeter [*or wherever the show is being performed*], we need you to listen carefully, for we have little time.

VAN HELSING. Exactly, so get on with it! Introduce me.

AL. I'd like to welcome to the stage…

VAN HELSING. I'm already on the stage, you idiot.

AL. The world's most renowned professor of sicko-kenny-isis.

VAN HELSING. Psychokinesis! Leave it, I'll introduce myself! Give me some light. Ladies and gentlemen and your offspring, my name is Professor Abraham Van Helsing. What you've just witnessed was a display of theatrical trickery – a fiction created with props. Tonight I need you to understand the difference between fiction and the truth. Wait, cut the music. What are you doing?

AL *is helping* DAN *fix a lamp on to a stand downstage left.*

DAN. Just finishing off with the lights, Professor.

VAN HELSING. You had all afternoon to finish off with the lights. What were you doing?

DAN. Giving him a massage –

VAN HELSING. What?

DAN. He tensed up a bit unpacking the set.

VAN HELSING. I've told you, it's not a set! It's furniture. From my house. God, I hate theatre! What's it for anyway?

AL. Your opening speech.

VAN HELSING. Oh right, I see. Well, plug it in then.

During VAN HELSING*'s following speech, the flex comes out of the lamp.* AL *shoves the bare wires back in.*

Ladies and gentlemen and your offspring, tonight you will discover that Bram Stoker's *Dracula*, is in fact… fact. Yes, fact! How do I know? Because that snake Stoker stole the events that happened to me and my friends and turned them into a fiction in a traitorous bid to further his own career. But I'm here to warn you of the true peril that still faces us all. This is *Dracula: The Bloody Truth* – direct from the horse's mouth!

Sound effect: neighing horses.

VAN HELSING. Not yet! Turn that off!

AL (*off*). Lamp is ready for plugging in, Professor.

VAN HELSING. Well, plug it in then! So, as I was saying…

The lamp explodes. The theatre blacks out.

DAN. Professor, the lights have gone out!

VAN HELSING. Yes, we can all see that, you buffoon! Get me a lamp! And find the trip-lever thing. Ladies and gentlemen, please stay in your seats, there's no need to panic.

MATT. I think I've found the lever.

AL (*crossing stage*). No, don't pull that one!

A sandbag drops from the rig and smashes through the table that the gramophone was on.

VAN HELSING. My Louis XIV! You've destroyed my Louis XIV!

DAN. To assist Professor Van Helsing in his mission to reconstruct the true events that happened to him and his friends, three versatile actors will step into the shoes of the men and women involved.

AL. It's this one.

He pulls the lever on the back wall. The lights come back on.

DAN. Professor, the lights are back on.

VAN HELSING. Oh, really? Thanks for letting me know because I hadn't noticed!

DAN. Really? Cos it's quite a contrast.

VAN HELSING. Just go and get ready with the horse and trap.

Sound effect: neighing horses.

Not yet! Ladies and gentlemen, please remember that what you will witness tonight should never be described as theatre.

You're here to be educated, not entertained. And a hundred and twenty years from now, in the year 2017, I hope that Bram Stoker will be remembered *only* as the charlatan he is.

A cart is wheeled on. A rocking horse with reins attached is placed in front of it.

Events began one night on the treacherous Borgo Pass, Transylvania, where a young solicitor called Jonathan Harker had been sent to complete some conveyancing work.

A place where even the mention of the name Borgo Pass spooked the horses. Horses. Now!

Sound effect: cows.

Horses!

VAN HELSING *exits with lamp through downstage-left door.*

Scene Three

Sound effect: horses, stormy. DRIVER *and his* WIFE *set off.*

HARKER. Wait! Please wait!

DRIVER. Whoa!! *Zdrah-stvoy.*

HARKER. Excuse me, do you speak English?

DRIVER. English? No, sorry, mate. 'Fraid not, mate.

HARKER. Oh. And how about your wife?

DRIVER. Do you speak English, mate?

WIFE. What are you saying?

DRIVER. I've no idea. We don't understand you, mate.

HARKER. Oh, for Christ's sake! I give you money, you take me in your cart. Yes?

WIFE. I think he wants to buy our cart.

DRIVER. He can take a piss in the lake with no shoes on, mate.

WIFE. Our cart is not for sale, darling.

HARKER. Listen, I don't think you're getting it! I give you money, I sit here. (*Sits on cart.*) And we go, yes?

WIFE. Ah!

HARKER. Do you understand?

WIFE. No, darling.

HARKER. Good. Dracula's castle please.

Sound effect: neighing horses. Thunder/lightning.

WIFE. Dracula's castle!? No. Those who venture there, never return.

HARKER. That's right. Dracula's castle.

WIFE. We can't take you there.

HARKER. Oh, I see, you want to haggle, do you? Another fifty?

WIFE. No, no!

HARKER. *Another* fifty?

WIFE. Stop offering us your money, darling.

HARKER. This is daylight robbery. Look, this is all I have.

DRIVER. Take the money, mate. We can buy a better horse. Yah!

The WIFE *takes his money and they set off.* HARKER *takes out his diary.*

HARKER. August 8th. The final leg of my journey to Count Dracula's castle took four hours.

DRIVER (*pointing*). Count Dracula's castle.

HARKER. But it seemed like less.

He jumps off the cart. WIFE *produces a crucifix.*

WIFE. Take this crucifix.

HARKER. No, I don't want to buy any of your Catholic wares, thank you.

WIFE *produces garlic.*

Or cooking ingredients.

WIFE *produces a wooden stake.*

And I definitely have no need for an oversized tent peg. Goodbye.

WIFE. Whatever you do, do not walk freely across his threshold!

HARKER. And the same to you.

He steps downstage.

So, this is Castle Dracula.

DRIVER *and* WIFE *attempt to exit with cart but the wheel is jammed.*

Now that I'm completely alone I must admit to feeling somewhat fearful. If only that couple were still here, I might ask for a lift back. But alas, they're now just a distant speck on the horizon.

VAN HELSING (*entering upstage*). Just lift it off!

They lift the cart back as curtains close. HARKER *approaches the stage-right door.*

Scene Four

HARKER. I suppose I have little choice but to knock.

Sound effect: door knocks, which the actor mistimes.
VAN HELSING*'s head emerges through curtains.*

VAN HELSING (*to tech box*). Not yet, he's still changing!

Sound effect: footsteps.

No! (*From behind curtain.*) Hurry up! He's at the door.

Sound effect: door creaks. A beat later VAN HELSING *opens the door.*

HARKER. Count Dracula?

VAN HELSING. Obviously not. No, he's just a little delayed.

Curtains open.

I suppose you may as well come in and wait.

DAN (*in wings*). Where are my shoes?

MATT (*in wings*). I don't know. Why did you take them off!?

DAN (*in wings*). I had an itchy toe.

VAN HELSING (*attempting to fill*). Let me take your coat.

HARKER. Thank you.

VAN HELSING *hangs* HARKER's *coat on a hook.*

And you must be…?

VAN HELSING. Nobody. Ignore me. And that horse.

He picks up the rocking horse that's been left on stage to strike it.

(*Into wings.*) Hurry up!

MATT (*from wings*). Just say the lines.

VAN HELSING. No!

DRACULA (*from wings*). Good evening. You must be Mr Harker?

HARKER. Yes.

VAN HELSING. Oh God.

DRACULA (*from wings*). Why are you looking at me like that? Am I not what you expected?

HARKER. You're just a little taller.

DRACULA (*from wings*). Before you enter, I must insist that you cross my threshold freely.

VAN HELSING. He's already in, you idiot!

DRACULA *finally enters* (*just changed*).

DRACULA. Ah. But I see you're already in.

HARKER. Yes. Your… *assistant* let me in.

VAN HELSING (*trying to leave*). He doesn't have an assistant!

DRACULA. I don't have an assistant.

HARKER. So it obviously wasn't him.

DRACULA. No, because I don't have an assistant.

HARKER. So it obviously wasn't him.

DRACULA. No, because I don't have an assistant.

HARKER. So it obviously wasn't him.

VAN HELSING. Oh, for goodness' sake, move on!

DRACULA. Let me take your coat.

> *They both clock* HARKER*'s coat, already hung up.*
> HARKER *hands it to* DRACULA.

VAN HELSING. Just skip forward!

DRACULA. Goodnight. (*Exiting with coat.*)

VAN HELSING. No, not that far! You must have had…?

DRACULA. You must have had –

HARKER (*comes in too early*). Yes, it's taken me four days to reach here.

DRACULA. – an interesting journey?

HARKER. Of wolves? No.

DRACULA. Are you frightened of wolves?

HARKER. I'm ravenous.

DRACULA. I expect you're hungry?

> *Pause.* DRACULA *hands coat back and exits.*

HARKER. I will be in a month or so.

DRACULA. Are you married?

HARKER. No. I'll gobble up anything you put in front of me though.

> DRACULA *enters with tray.*

DRACULA. Have you ever tried horse meat? I prepared it earlier.

HARKER *looks out front from hanging coat.*

HARKER. Three hundred years ago!? How is that possible?

DRACULA. I see you're looking at my portrait. It was painted in 1597.

HARKER. Do I?

DRACULA. You seem nervous.

VAN HELSING. For Pete's sake, just tell him to sit down.

DRACULA. Sit down, Pete. Mr Harker.

HARKER *sits.* DRACULA *places tray and pours some wine.*

Your good health.

HARKER (*reaching for bag*). I've brought the conveyancing papers.

DRACULA. Eat!

HARKER *obeys and is about to eat.*

Did you bring the conveyancing papers?

HARKER. Yes, here in my...

DRACULA. Eat! It's time for me to move on from this place, you see. I only hope this new property in England will suit my requirements.

HARKER. Oh, I think you'll like it.

HARKER *takes his first mouthful as* DRACULA *takes fork from him.*

DRACULA. Good. And now, since you've finished eating, I'll show you to your room. We can continue with our business tomorrow night.

HARKER. Or in the morning perhaps?

DRACULA. That won't be possible. I'll be away from the castle all day.

HARKER. Well, all I really need is your signature, then I can be on my way.

DRACULA. Do you have a pen?

HARKER. Yes.

DRACULA. Until tomorrow night then. Your room is that way.

He looks up violently. Then slowly back at HARKER, *who picks up his bag and starts to exit.*

Finish your wine.

HARKER *drinks under* DRACULA's *insistent gaze with accompanying sound effects. He then continues to exit stage left.*

Oh, what's this you've dropped?

DRACULA *attempts to shake a 'palmed' photo from his sleeve.*

HARKER. Ah. It's a photograph of my fiancée, Mina. It must have fallen from my pocket there on to the floor.

DRACULA (*attempting to retrieve it from further up his sleeve*). Yes, I'm trying to pick it up for you. She's very beautiful. She reminds me of a woman I once knew.

He eventually yanks the crumpled photo out, drops it on floor and picks it up.

You should keep this safe.

HARKER. I will.

DRACULA. Someone so special.

HARKER (*dreamy*). Sometimes it feels like destiny brought us together.

He turns to exit, DRACULA *is in his path.*

DRACULA. And I feel the same way about you too... Mr Harker.

They exit. Curtains close. VAN HELSING *enters through door.*

VAN HELSING. You want to get up and shake him, don't you? 'Get out! Get out of there now, you idiot!' But what you have to understand is that the moment Jonathan Harker freely entered that castle, he fell under a spell.

Scene Five

HARKER *is in bed with his diary.*

HARKER. 3 a.m. Haven't slept a wink. It seems as if the castle itself is alive.

Sound effect: breaths. He produces MINA's *ripped photo.*

Oh, Mina. I miss you so much. (*Beat.*) Perhaps a shave will help me sleep.

He gets up and opens the cupboard and begins to shave. He cuts himself and turns away towards his bag. DRACULA *suddenly appears in the mirror, then disappears by the time* HARKER *turns back.* DRACULA *then appears from around the side of the cupboard.*

DRACULA. That cut will need attending to.

DRACULA *leans towards* HARKER *then lurches for his neck.*

HARKER. What are you doing!?

DRACULA. I might ask the same of you – getting up to shave in the middle of the night!

HARKER. I insist on being left alone!

DRACULA. Of course. Please excuse me. I shall leave you to… sleep well.

He exits into the cupboard and closes the doors.

HARKER. Excuse me, but you can't just…

HARKER *opens the cupboard, expecting it to be empty.*

Disappear!?

But DRACULA *hasn't quite disappeared so he repeats the action.*

Disappear!?

With the cupboard now empty, he steps inside to examine mirror. The doors automatically close.

Curtains close.

VAN HELSING. You think we're making this up!? You think this is fiction? No! This is what actually happened. And I'm not talking about a trick cupboard like that one. Inside the walls of Dracula's castle, the rules of logic and reason were rewritten.

Curtains open. Empty stage. HARKER *is stood looking bewildered.*

HARKER. Hello? How did I end up in the corridor?

Blackout. HARKER *strikes a match. It goes out. He lights another. A* BRIDE *appears upstage left (in prosthetic mask) but* HARKER *doesn't see her. She disappears from light then reappears downstage right.*

Who are you!? I'm sorry, I need to get out of here.

BRIDE 1. Surely, Jonathan…

Second BRIDE *appears.*

BRIDE 2. Jonathan…

Third BRIDE *appears.*

BRIDE 3. Jonathan…

BRIDE 2. You're not going to deny us the pleasure…

BRIDE 1. Pleasure…

BRIDE 3. Pleasure… of your company.

BRIDE 2. We're desperate…

BRIDE 1. Desperate.

BRIDE 2. Desperate.

BRIDE 1. For you.

BRIDE 2. For you.

BRIDE 1 *and* 2 *approach and caress him.*

HARKER. Was I aroused? Absolutely… not! No… no… no… NO!!

He escapes downstage.

What were those fearful creatures? Slaves to Count Dracula? I need to get back to my room. This will all make sense in the morning... won't it?

He turns upstage and walks into DRACULA, *whose voice is amplified.*

DRACULA. Mr Harker, did I not insist that you shouldn't go exploring the castle!

HARKER. I've been looking for my room.

DRACULA. All day!?

HARKER. What?

DRACULA. Supper is served.

HARKER. Supper!? But... I have to leave!

DRACULA. Before you have my signature? That won't do, surely?

HARKER. The papers are in my room.

DRACULA. Are they not in your case?

HARKER suddenly notices that his case is now in his hand.

HARKER. How the hell did...?

DRACULA. Are you feeling all right, Mr Harker?

HARKER. Listen! All I need you to do is sign here.

He takes out contract.

BRIDE 1. Jonathan.

DRACULA. Get away from him.

DRACULA makes her 'disappear' through the back wall (a cat flap, effectively).

It seems we'll need to reconvene tomorrow night.

HARKER. But how do I even get back to my room? What's happened to the doors?

DRACULA. The doors? They're all here, Mr Harker.

He drags on screen (with three doors).

Here is one, and here is another.

He exits through it and then continues to pull the screen on to centre stage (but there's been a switch).

(*His voice remains amplified.*) I suggest preparing a letter to your employer to say that you might be indefinitely delayed.

His hand beckons through a screen door.

This way, Mr Harker.

HARKER. Now look here!

BRIDE 1 *steps out, downstage left.*

BRIDE 1. Jonathan.

DRACULA *appears downstage right.*

DRACULA. Get away from him!

BRIDE 2 *steps through door.*

BRIDE 2. Jonathan.

DRACULA. Away from him! He's mine.

BRIDES *exit.*

Mr Harker, I have your signed contract.

HARKER (*taking it*). Which is the way out!?

DRACULA. Relax. I posted your letter to your employer today.

HARKER. What letter?

DRACULA. Your letter. Explaining that you won't be home for a month or so!

HARKER. I didn't write a letter!?

DRACULA. You seem very confused. Goodnight.

He exits through a screen door. HARKER *steps downstage.*

HARKER. I began drafting a letter to Mina, telling her of the horrors of this place and that she must send help to get me out of here. But how would I get the letter to her?

A PEASANT *enters from downstage left.*

You there. I need you to take this letter to a postbox. It's imperative. Please!

PEASANT. Of course I will…

He takes letter and exits through screen door. DRACULA enters through another door with the letter.

DRACULA.…Mr Harker!

HARKER. No!!

Curtains close.

Scene Six

Front cloth – a train station. MINA is sat on her case, writing.

MINA. My dear Jonathan. Two months now and only a rather odd letter from you to inform me you are detained in Transylvania. I'm finding your absence unbearable. So I'm travelling to Whitby to stay with my dear friend, Lucy.

CONDUCTOR. Whitby. Final call!

MINA jigs along to train-journey lighting effects and music. Her case falls open, spilling the contents.

Whitby. This is Whitby!

LUCY enters.

LUCY. Mina!

MINA. Lucy!

Over dialogue, they gather up the spilled contents and throw the case and all into the downstage wings.

LUCY. Oh, how I have missed you. We have so much catching up to do. Let's get back home.

Scene Seven

Curtains open to LUCY*'s residence. Chaise longue, Victorian three-panel screen (with three doors cut into it), small Louis XIV table (now with a hole through it). Sound effect of the train is still running so they have to shout.*

MINA (*shouting*). I can't tell you what a relief it is to be out of London, Lucy.

LUCY (*shouting*). I can imagine.

MINA (*shouting*). It couldn't be more quiet and tranquil here.

LUCY (*shouting*). Yes, I love it!

MINA (*shouting*). So you aren't still finding it…

Sound effect of the train stops.

So you aren't still finding it incessantly boring?

She sits on chaise longue, which collapses at downstage end. They try to ignore it.

What is it, Lucy? You're hiding something.

LUCY. Mina, I have a suitor.

MINA. Oh, Lucy, I insist that you sit beside me and tell me all about him.

LUCY *sits and can't prevent slipping into* MINA.

LUCY. Well, to be honest, there are three men who wish to marry me.

MINA. Three?

LUCY. That doesn't make me a wanton creature with a ravenous sexual appetite, does it?

MINA. Of course not! You're a strong and intelligent woman who happens to possess a body to die for. Of course you're going to get multiple offers.

LUCY. Well, others might think differently.

MINA (*standing*). You mean, people like the novelist, Bram Stoker!? Who choose to present women like you as symbols of immorality?

VAN HELSING (*through downstage-left door*). The gall of the man – presenting my dear friend Lucy in that way. What have you done to my chaise longue!

MINA. So, what will you do?

LUCY. Oh, Mina, it's so hard to decide between them.

MRS WESTENRA (*off*). Lucy!?

LUCY. In the morning room, Mother.

MINA. Is your mother still as batty as ever?

LUCY. Getting worse, I'm afraid.

MRS WESTENRA (*played by* DAN) *enters*.

MRS WESTENRA. Ah. You're in here then.

LUCY. Yes. What was it you wanted?

MRS WESTENRA. Wanted?

LUCY. You were looking for me.

MRS WESTENRA. When!?

LUCY. Just now.

MRS WESTENRA. Just now? No, I was answering the front door just now.

LUCY. Who to?

MRS WESTENRA. That's right.

LUCY. Who was at the door, Mother?

MRS WESTENRA. What door?

LUCY. The front door. Who was it?

MRS WESTENRA. Shall I show him in?

LUCY. Who? Who is it!?

MRS WESTENRA. Dr Seward.

LUCY. Dr Seward?

MRS WESTENRA. I'll make some tea.

She exits.

LUCY. Oh, goodness.

MINA. What is it?

LUCY. Dr Seward is one of my three suitors.

MINA. A doctor? How exciting.

LUCY. Yes, he's in charge of a psychiatric hospital in Essex.

MINA. That's mental.

LUCY. It's crazy, isn't it? But just *before* he comes in though,
Mina...

   SEWARD *enters too early.*

SEWARD. Lucy!

LUCY (*forcefully loud*). I must just tell you that...

SEWARD (*realising his mistake*). Ah.

   He tries to exit but the door is stuck. VAN HELSING
   appears around side of screen.

VAN HELSING. Get off. She's got to finish the line first.

SEWARD. I know.

LUCY (*talking very slowly*)....if he should ask me to
mmmmmm...

VAN HELSING. Just go around!

   DAN *exits round screen.*

LUCY....marry him, I will turn him down. Ah, this sounds like
him now.

   SEWARD *tries to enter but door is still stuck.* VAN
   HELSING *comes to front of screen and tries to open it from
   stage side before returning behind screen.*

VAN HELSING (*off*). Just go around!

SEWARD. Right.

   SEWARD *comes around side of screen just as* VAN
   HELSING *finally bursts the door open.*

It smacks SEWARD *in the face (which* VAN HELSING *doesn't notice).*

VAN HELSING (*thumbs-up*). Door's fixed.

LUCY. Dr Seward, what a lovely surprise.

SEWARD *has a full-on nosebleed, which drips onto the daffodils he's holding.*

You're looking ever so well.

SEWARD. I've never felt better.

LUCY. And what beautiful daffodils you've brought.

SEWARD. Yes. I remembered they were your favourite. Here.

LUCY. Oh, you shouldn't have. Aren't they lovely, Mina?

MINA. They're gorgeous.

LUCY. Could you go and ask Mother to bring in a vase with the tea?

MINA. Of course.

VAN HELSING *appears.*

VAN HELSING (*sotto to* MINA). Get a mop and bucket to clean up this blood.

LUCY. Have a seat, Dr Seward.

SEWARD. Thank you. Won't you come and sit beside me?

They sit on the broken chaise longue.

LUCY. How is the mental asylum you run in Essex?

SEWARD. I'm dealing closely with a man called Renfield, who's obsessed with eating insects.

LUCY. He sounds crazy.

SEWARD. He is. Just like I'm crazy about you, Lucy. I came here because there's something I want to ask you.

LUCY. Ah, here's Mother with the tea.

MRS WESTENRA (*now played by* MATT) *enters with mop and bucket.*

SEWARD. Let me take that tray from you, Mrs Westenra.

He takes the mop.

LUCY. Place it on the table if you would, Dr Seward.

He places it through *the table just as* VAN HELSING *enters*.

VAN HELSING. Give that here.

He grabs mop and bucket and starts mopping.

LUCY. This is our new cleaner.

VAN HELSING. No it isn't! Ignore me! Just go and get the tea.

SEWARD *starts to exit*. VAN HELSING *herds him back with mop*.

Not you! Him.

MRS WESTENRA *exits. Sound effect: doorbell.*

LUCY. I wonder who that can be?

Screen door opens.

MRS WESTENRA. Lucy? There's another man at the door.

LUCY. Who is it?

MRS WESTENRA. That's right.

LUCY. Who's at the door, Mother?

MRS WESTENRA. Quincey Morris. I'll show him in.

She exits.

LUCY (*referring to* VAN HELSING). No, don't show him in yet. I think he might be a bit busy.

VAN HELSING. No he isn't. He won't be a moment.

He hands LUCY *the mop* (*but leaves bucket in front of screen*) *before exiting.*

SEWARD. Now look here, Lucy, before old Quincey comes in, there's something I'd like to ask you. The thing is –

LUCY. Here's Mother with the tea. Watch the bucket!

MRS WESTENRA (*still played by* MATT) *enters with tray and trips over the bucket. The contents of the tray fly.*

SEWARD (*picking up the teapot*). Here. Let me take that tray from you, Mrs Westenra.

LUCY. Just place it over there on the table, if you wouldn't mind, Dr Seward.

SEWARD places teapot on Louis XIV table with hole in it. Unsurprisingly, it falls through and smashes. Sound effect: doorbell.

Mother, could you go and see who's at the door, please?

MRS WESTENRA (*heading out*). Of course.

Door opens and smacks her in the face.

LUCY. Pass your cup, Doctor, and I'll pour.

SEWARD. Lovely.

Since there is no teapot, LUCY is obliged to pour the contents of the mop bucket into SEWARD's cup.

Now, Lucy. As I was saying…

MRS WESTENRA (MATT) *enters.*

MRS WESTENRA. Mr Quincey Morris.

QUINCEY (*entering*). Howdee.

LUCY. Quincey, how wonderful to see you. Mother, could you see where Mina's got to – (*Handing her the bucket.*) and make some fresh tea?

MATT (*exhausted*). Seriously?

He exits.

QUINCEY. I hope you don't mind me dropping in like this, Lucy?

LUCY. Not at all. You remember Dr Seward?

QUINCEY. Good to see you again, Doctor.

LUCY. Tea?

QUINCEY. You know I never can refuse a cup of good old Rosie Lee.

LUCY *takes the cup (with liquid from bucket) from*
SEWARD *and hands it to* QUINCEY.

SEWARD (*sotto, alarmed*). Not that one!

QUINCEY. I wondered if I might have a moment alone with
you, Lucy.

LUCY. Alone?

QUINCEY. After I've finished my tea, of course.

MINA *enters, and* QUINCEY, *not realising the danger,*
takes a mouthful.

LUCY. Quincey, this is my best friend, Mina.

QUINCEY *spits out foul liquid into* MINA'*s face and begins*
to retch. MINA *takes* LUCY *aside.*

MINA. Lucy, Arthur Holmwood's in the kitchen, he's come to
propose.

LUCY. They all have. But it's Arthur I want to marry.

MINA. I'll keep him occupied. You faint.

LUCY. Perfect.

MINA *exits.* LUCY *faints.*

SEWARD. Lucy! I'll deal with this. I've got some smelling
salts in my bag.

QUINCEY *pukes into* SEWARD'*s bag.*

I'll just fetch them.

SEWARD *takes out smelling salts, dripping in vomit.*

Take a deep breath of this, Lucy.

LUCY '*comes round', trying not to retch.*

LUCY. What happened?

SEWARD. You fainted. Here, let me help you up.

She recoils from his pukey hand.

LUCY. I need to go and lie down.

SEWARD. Quincey, get the door, will you?

They all exit.

MINA (*off*). Just wait in here, Mr Holmwood. Help yourself to tea.

HOLMWOOD *enters.*

HOLMWOOD. Right you are.

LUCY *enters.* VAN HELSING *ushers them both downstage in order to close the curtains behind them.*

LUCY. Arthur, how lovely to see you.

HOLMWOOD. And you, Lucy.

LUCY. To what do I owe the pleasure?

HOLMWOOD. Well, since we're alone, I'd like to ask you a question.

LUCY. Yes?

HOLMWOOD. Will you marry me?

LUCY. Oh, Arthur! Yes, yes I will.

This is normally the end of the scene but VAN HELSING *sticks his head through curtain.*

VAN HELSING. We're still clearing up. Add some lines.

LUCY. What's your favourite kind of… pheasant?

HOLMWOOD. The feathery ones. How long have you been growing your hair?

LUCY. Since I was born. You?

VAN HELSING. All right, that'll do. We're ready. Go now. Go.

HOLMWOOD *and* LUCY *exit through the stage-left door.* VAN HELSING *steps through curtains.*

Ladies and gentlemen, we now travel to the dockyards, Gdańsk, Poland. Why? Because that's where Dracula was at this moment. How do I know? Because this is the Captain's logbook from the *Demeter* – the cargo ship that he boarded.

Scene Eight

Sound effect: docks. Curtains open to reveal a tea chest on top of another.

VOICE (*off*). Hurry up and get those boxes loaded. We set sail in an hour!

DOCK WORKER (*entering*). *Da, da.* I'm going as fast as I can!

He picks up top tea chest and reveals DRACULA.

DRACULA. Is that the boat to Whitby?

DOCK WORKER. Might be. Who's asking?

DRACULA. I am. I want to transport some... boxes to England.

DOCK WORKER. What kind of boxes?

DRACULA. Person-sized.

DOCK WORKER. What, coffins, are they?

DRACULA. No, person-sized.

DOCK WORKER. How many?

DRACULA. Fifty.

DOCK WORKER. Fifty!? No can do, mate. More than my job's worth. This boat's already up to capacity.

DRACULA. I will pay you well.

DOCK WORKER. Fifty empty boxes?

DRACULA. Not exactly empty.

DOCK WORKER. Why, what's in 'em? Bodies?

DRACULA. No! Just... earth.

DOCK WORKER. Earth!?

DRACULA. Yes. Soil.

DOCK WORKER. What are you, some sort of gardener?

DRACULA. Yes, correct. I am just some sort of gardener. A very wealthy some sort of gardener. Follow me.

They exit.

VAN HELSING. The boxes were loaded aboard, unbeknownst the Captain and crew. The *Demeter* set sail.

Scene Nine

Sound effect: a ship at sea. MATT *runs on, waving a sheet on a rope.*

VAN HELSING. For ten days… what are you doing? Stop the music. What the hell are you doing?

MATT. Representing the ship.

VAN HELSING. They know we're on a ship. I've just told them. How is you waving that about helping?

MATT. I thought it would look like a sail.

VAN HELSING. Oh, you think this looks like a sail, do you? And this bit of rope?

MATT. The rigging?

VAN HELSING. Oh, the rigging. How clever. I'll tell you what it looks like. A piece of sheet! Christ, I hate theatre. And actors. Get off and take your pissy sheet-on-a-rope with you.

He turns to AL, *who is hiding a sheet behind his back.*

And what are you doing? Have you got a pissy sheet-on-a-rope too?

AL. No. It's hers.

He throws the sheet into the front row and exits.

VAN HELSING. Right, we all know we're on a ship. Just play the damn sound effect.

Sound effect: horse.

No! The sea! Play the sea!

Sound effect: a ship at sea.

The *Demeter* set sail. For ten days there was nothing of interest to report. But then things started to change.

CAPTAIN *enters and sits on remaining tea chest.*

'Captain's log. Day ten. Crew member Dainton has gone missing.

CAPTAIN. A tall thin man has been spotted.' Where did you see this man, First Mate?

FIRST MATE. On the port bow, Captain. But there's no sign of him now.

CAPTAIN. Search the ship!

VAN HELSING. The ship was searched for five hours.

FIRST MATE. No sign of the stowaway.

VAN HELSING. 'Captain's log. Day thirteen.

FIRST MATE. Another crew member has disappeared.'

CAPTAIN. What!? Men don't just disappear.

FIRST MATE. The crew are feeling very nervous, Captain.

CAPTAIN. Search the ship again.

VAN HELSING. 'Day fifteen. Another three crew members are missing.

CAPTAIN. The men are numb with fear and the first mate has started to go mad.'

FIRST MATE (*singing*). 'I'm Mummy's little soldier and I'm not scared…'

DRACULA (*from wings*). Good evening. I expect you're wondering what's going on…

FIRST MATE. No, no, no!

VAN HELSING. 'Captain's log. Day sixteen.

CAPTAIN. Just four crew members remain and the ship's engineer – '

ENGINEER (*off*). Arggh!

CAPTAIN. ' – has thrown himself overboard!'

VAN HELSING. 'Captain's log, day eighteen.

CAPTAIN. One day from Whitby. I am the only soul left on board and we're heading into a storm… I am going to lash myself to the wheel and attempt to bring us in.'

VAN HELSING. From the cliff, in Whitby, crowds gathered and watched in horror.

Scene Ten

Whitby cliff. [DAD *and* SON *are played by the same actor.*]

SON. Eh, Dad, look! There's someone tied tut wheel! Save their souls.

DAD. She'll be smashed ont' rocks.

SON. No, she's missed rocks. It's a bloody miracle. She's gonna beach. What's that ont' deck? Some kind of dog?

DAD. I ain't never seen a dog that size.

SON. It's leapt on tut beach, Dad.

DAD. That's not a dog.

SON. What the bloody heck's going on?

VAN HELSING. Exactly, what the bloody heck was going on? But Lucy and Mina? They were oblivious of anything untoward.

Scene Eleven

LUCY *and* MINA, *carrying parasols, are strolling along the promenade in Whitby. Paper seagulls fly by.*

MINA. Lucy, it's so exciting – you getting married.

LUCY. Oh, I know. And have you and Jonathan set a date yet?

MINA *starts to cry.*

Mina, what is it?

MINA. I expect I'm just over-worrying. But I haven't heard from Jonathan for over a month now.

LUCY. I'm sure it's nothing. You know what conveyancing's like.

MINA. No. (*Beat.*) But I'm sure you're right. It's probably nothing.

VAN HELSING. Of course it wasn't nothing!! Jonathan Harker was trapped in Dracula's castle! But how could anyone have known that? And where was I? In my laboratory in Amsterdam, frustratingly still not in the story yet.

MINA. At least being here in Whitby with you calms my nerves.

LUCY. Yes. Nothing ever happens here.

MINA. Goodness! What's all that commotion on the beach?

LUCY. It looks like a ship run aground on the sand.

A BLOKE *approaches.*

Excuse me, sir, what's going on here?

BLOKE. Russian cargo ship. Came through storm last night with her sails fully hoisted.

DRACULA *appears next to* LUCY. MINA *doesn't notice him.*

DRACULA. Like some ungodly force were controlling her.

MINA. Gosh! And the crew?

BLOKE. They only found the Captain, lashed to the wheel.

DRACULA. With a crucifix in his hand.

MINA. Alive?

BLOKE. Dead.

DRACULA. With a look of terror upon his face.

LUCY. How shocking.

BLOKE. Then a great dog-like creature leapt off the deck, bigger than a wolf with bright-red eyes. I've got to go.

He exits.

LUCY. Well, thank you both very much for the information.

DRACULA *exits.*

MINA. Both?

LUCY. Yes. Him and… the man who was stood right beside me.

MINA. There wasn't anyone else stood beside you, Lucy.

Sound effect: sting. BOX MAN enters with a 2D cut-out of a coffin.

BOX MAN. Watch your backs, ladies. Boxes of earth coming through.

MINA. Boxes of earth?

BOX MAN. Yes, love. Fifty coffin-shaped boxes of earth unloaded off the *Demeter*, all to be delivered to Carfax Abbey in Essex.

MINA. That's a lot of information in one sentence.

BOX MAN (*beat*). Yep.

He exits.

MINA. This is all rather odd, isn't it?

LUCY. Yes, it is, in a way. But then again, it isn't in a way. Mina, you're such a worry-puss.

MINA. Oh, you're probably right, Lucy. I am being a silly worry-puss.

Sound effect: Punch and Judy show that gets progressively freaky-sounding (Punch laughing).

LUCY (*towards front*). Oh, look! A Punch and Judy show!

MINA. Wait here. I'll go and get us an ice cream.

She exits.

LUCY (*into wing*). One deckchair please?

Deckchair is handed in from the wings. LUCY *sits to watch the show.* DRACULA *walks up behind her. He passes her an ice cream and places a hand on her shoulder.*

(*Placing her hand on* DRACULA's *hand.*) Thank you, Mina. I feel so close to you.

DRACULA *exits. Danger sound effects fade.* MINA *enters with two ice creams.*

MINA. Here we go.

LUCY. Another?

MINA. Where did you get that?

LUCY. You just gave it to me.

MINA. No I didn't. I've only just returned.

LUCY. Then who gave me this and stroked my hair?

Sound effect: sting.

What is it, Mina?

MINA. I don't know. But I think we should go home.

Curtains close.

VAN HELSING. Are you beginning to see now, people of Exeter? He can make his presence known to some and not others. These are the supernatural forces we're up against. Count Dracula now had Miss Lucy in his sights. We travel now to Lucy Westenra's house. Picture the scene. It's the dead of night. A full moon hangs in the sky. The crickets hum.

Scene Twelve

Curtains open. A sash window frame is hanging downstage left.
MINA *and* LUCY *asleep in the bed upstage right.*

VAN HELSING. Everyone fast asleep. Seems peaceful, doesn't
it? Serene, you might say. Was it? No it was not! There were
supernatural forces at work.

LUCY *sits up in a trance.*

Look! See how Miss Lucy rose up, awoken by some dark
force. See the hunger, the lust in her eyes. If only I had been
there. But I'm still not in the damn story yet. It's like I'm
trapped in a glass case, unable to communicate.

*He imitates being trapped in a glass case, with muted
shouting towards* LUCY.

You know, with the glass walls and the ceiling? So she can't
hear me! You understand… Ah, just forget it! As she reaches
the window, it opens by itself. The window… pull the rope!

The rope snaps and the window frame almost hits the floor.

(*To* MINA.) Go and help with the window. Just hold it.

MATT *and* DAN *hold the frame between them while* DAN
lifts the sash open.

Through the open window she glided.

LUCY *reaches the window.* DAN *accidentally drops the
sash section, which slams down on* LUCY's *fingers.* DAN
lifts the sash to free them.

Just walk around it.

LUCY *tries to continue as normal.* DAN *exits and sash
drops onto* MATT's *fingers.* AL/LUCY *lifts sash to free him.*

She began walking towards the graveyard on the cliff that
overlooked Whitby. And where was Mina? Still in bed.

MINA *is getting back into bed but still holding window
frame.*

Not with the window! Go to sleep!

He takes window and places it stage right.

A strange, dark shadow watched Miss Lucy as she entered the graveyard.

DRACULA *appears*.

It was like he was there, but also like he wasn't.

DRACULA *exits, thinking that's a stage direction*.

No, what are you doing? Come back. Just stand there! He was present but not present.

He again misunderstands and starts to exit.

No, stay there! Lucy was sat…

LUCY, *still in trance, is dragging a chair downstage with her foot*.

Who didn't set the chair?

AL (LUCY). It wasn't my fault.

VAN HELSING. Shut up, you're in a trance. Just sit there.

He sets chair downstage centre and pushes LUCY/AL *into it*.

Lucy was sat like a sitting duck, unaware of what lay before her.

But meanwhile, Mina had awoken from her slumber. She notices Lucy isn't beside her. Bigger reaction. No, smaller than that.

VAN HELSING *grabs a gramophone horn and starts directing the scene* (*like a film director*).

Wait… Wait… that's it. Now see the open window. Where's the window?

DRACULA (*picking it up*). Here.

VAN HELSING. No! You're Dracula. Get back over there!

VAN HELSING takes the window from him and holds it up.

Mina ran to the window and looked out.

MINA. Lucy!

VAN HELSING. But the wind drowned out her voice. More wind. I need more wind!

Sound effect: wind increases.

She knew she had to go after her.

MINA *tries to climb out of the window that* VAN HELSING *is holding.*

What are you doing? Why would she climb out of a window!? Just use the front door, man.

MINA *enters through stage-left door and runs on the spot.* VAN HELSING *returns to using horn.*

She ran all the way along the cliff until she reached the graveyard. And there she saw Lucy. But there was something else – a dark tall figure leant over her friend.

MINA. Lucy!

DRACULA *looks up.*

VAN HELSING. Not that fast, Dracula. Slowly, take your time, more face, less face. She doesn't actually see you! All right, that'll do. Go.

DRACULA *exits.*

Mina approaches. And line.

MINA. Lucy, my darling, why are you out here at this hour?

LUCY. Where am I? I feel so weak.

VAN HELSING (*getting into the drama*). Good.

MINA. You're stone cold. Here, take my shawl. Let's get you back home.

VAN HELSING. This is perfect.

MINA *wraps a shawl around* LUCY.

LUCY. I'm so sleepy…

MINA. What are these marks on your neck? I must have just pricked you with my shawl pin – yes, that's it.

VAN HELSING. A shawl pin!? A shawl pin!? No! She had been bitten by Count Dracula and was about to fall under his spell.

MINA *leads* LUCY *back to the bed.*

Scene Thirteen

MINA. She doesn't look well. I shall call for Dr Seward first thing in the morning.

Sound effect: a cockerel. SEWARD *enters.*

SEWARD. Good morning. I received your message.

MINA. She seems to be sleeping peacefully now, Doctor.

SEWARD. Let me take a look – (*Without looking.*) My God, this woman needs a doctor.

MINA. That's why I called you.

SEWARD. And that's why I'm here.

He rummages through his bag.

Slow heart rate, low blood pressure and my God, she feels cold to the touch…

MINA. What does it all mean?

He stands up with stethoscope.

SEWARD. I've no idea. And these two marks on her neck.

He turns to look at her neck.

MINA. I think I caused them with my shawl pin.

SEWARD. Don't be so ridiculous. It looks like a bite mark.

MINA. But what could have bitten her? A bird? A snake? (*Beat.*) A goat?

SEWARD. There's no point just randomly naming creatures, Mina. This needs a more methodical approach. Pass me that glossary of animals.

A book is thrown from the wings.

MINA. This one?

SEWARD. Exactly. (*Opens book.*) Aardvark, no; aardwolf, unlikely; addax, no idea what that is...

MINA. Could it have been a bat?

SEWARD. A bat? My God.

MINA. What is it?

SEWARD. Basically, a mouse with wings. I must send a telegram immediately.

MINA. Who to?

SEWARD. To the most intelligent, brilliant –

VAN HELSING (*from wings*). Respected.

SEWARD. Respected –

VAN HELSING (*from wings*). Undervalued.

SEWARD. Undervalued man I know. Professor Abraham Van Helsing.

MINA. Is he a... batman?

SEWARD. Something like that. I have to go.

He exits.

VAN HELSING. And where was I? In Amsterdam, giving a lecture on iron deficiency in newts.

He takes a step. Spotlight appears beside him, not lighting him.

Anaemia was removed as a variable by adjusting the haemoglobin, et cetera, et cetera, blah, blah, blah.

SEWARD *hands him a telegram.*

A telegram from my old student, C-Word? Thank you, C-Word. (*Reads.*) Smoking windmills. Apologies, class, I must travel to Whitby immediately.

He exits through the door as SEWARD *enters through screen door.*

MINA. She's not looking good. How long do you think it will take your professor of si-chicken-esis –

VAN HELSING (*bursting in*). Psychokinesis!

MINA. – to get here?

VAN HELSING. Finally I'm in the story. Where's the patient?

SEWARD. Here on the bed.

VAN HELSING (*to* MINA). You, I'm going to need some garlic.

MINA. I'll go and find Mrs Westenra.

She exits.

VAN HELSING. You did the right thing in calling me, Seward.

SEWARD. How can I assist you?

VAN HELSING. Close that window immediately.

SEWARD. Yes, Professor.

SEWARD *picks up the sash window and turns it upside down so the sash drops.* VAN HELSING *is unpacking his 'blood transfusion' kit.*

VAN HELSING. This woman needs a blood transfusion straight away. Who knows her breast? Best. Best breast. Ah, tits.

SEWARD. Well, her fiancé is a man called...

HOLMWOOD (*entering*). Arthur Holmwood. What's going on?

VAN HELSING. Remove your jacket.

SEWARD *pulls* HOLMWOOD*'s jacket off.*

Now, roll up your sleeve and shit down, shit down, ah, crap. And where's Mrs Westenra with the garlic?

SEWARD (*exiting*). I'll go and find her.

HOLMWOOD. What's this all about?

VAN HELSING. I'm trying to shave, SAVE your fiancée.

He sticks a pipe from the kit into HOLMWOOD*'s arm. Blood from the other end starts spurting out, forcing*

VAN HELSING *to put it in his mouth before getting it into* LUCY*'s arm.* MRS WESTENRA (DAN) *enters with garlic.*

MRS WESTENRA. What's going on? Why have I brought this in?

VAN HELSING (*taking garlic*). The garlic must be placed around her neck.

MRS WESTENRA. Around her neck? It'll stink the room out. I'll open that window.

She turns window upside down.

VAN HELSING. No! It's imperative that you keep that window closed at all times.

She considers turning window back the other way but it's a real effort.

MRS WESTENRA. Ah, feck it.

VAN HELSING. And where's Seward got to?

MRS WESTENRA (*exiting*). I'll go and find him.

HOLMWOOD. Why must we keep the window closed, Professor? What's happened to Lucy?

VAN HELSING. If I told you, you wouldn't believe me.

HOLMWOOD. I don't believe you.

VAN HELSING. Very well. At this moment, Lucy is in grave danger of becoming…

HOLMWOOD. What?

VAN HELSING. One of the living dead.

HOLMWOOD. The living dead?

SEWARD enters, reading from another glossary.

SEWARD. Creepers, empties, flesh-dolls –

VAN HELSING. Yes, thank you, Seward.

SEWARD. Lurkers, mush-brains, swivel-heads –

VAN HELSING. Thank you, Doctor! I'm talking about
vampires. And I believe that Lucy is in the grip of the
godfather of them all.

HOLMWOOD. Oh, come on, this all sounds very...

VAN HELSING. Sexual?! Maybe in the early stages, and in the
middle and quite a bit towards the end actually but ultimately
the only way to release a victim's trapped soul is to... well,
I'm not going to get explicit... but is to hammer a stake
through their heart and cut off their head.

HOLMWOOD. You're insane.

VAN HELSING. Am I?

HOLMWOOD. I don't know.

SEWARD. He's not!

VAN HELSING. Can you afford not to take me seriously?

SEWARD. No, he can't!

VAN HELSING. We have to prevent him from making contact
with Lucy again.

SEWARD *grabs* HOLMWOOD *by the collar and pulls him
to his feet.*

SEWARD. For God's sake, man, take him seriously!

VAN HELSING. Seward, calm down! Go and take a cold
shower!

SEWARD *exits.* VAN HELSING *pulls tube out of*
HOLMWOOD'*s arm. Sound effect: suction pop.*

Typically, the victim won't remember anything that's
occurred. And we should keep it that way – for her own sake.

LUCY *sits up.*

LUCY. Arthur? What are you doing here? And who's he?

HOLMWOOD. You were taken sick, Lucy. But this man...

VAN HELSING. Professor Abraham Van Helsing.

HOLMWOOD. Has made you better.

VAN HELSING. And now you must rest. And I must leave you for a short while.

He exits but returns around side of screen.

But while I'm gone, whatever you do, don't remove the garlic, don't fall asleep and keep the windows shut.

He exits, and returns again, moving downstage.

Scene Fourteen

VAN HELSING. The biggest mistake of my life? Leaving the house that night. He was there. He was everywhere. But where was he? He was nowhere. He was like a shadow.

He pulls on a small screen on wheels. DRACULA (behind) casts a classic Dracula shadow.

A shadow that doesn't exist.

He pulls the screen further onstage, revealing DRACULA holding the pose before he darts into the wings.

All that idiot Holmwood had to do was stay awake.

VAN HELSING *places the window on the frame.* HOLMWOOD *brings a chair to sit behind it, casting a shadow.*

That's all he had to do! Stay awake, you fool!

He slaps the sheet as shadow of HOLMWOOD *falls asleep.* HOLMWOOD *hits him back through the sheet.*

And it didn't take long before Mrs Westenra came in.

MATT *realises that's his cue line for* MRS WESTENRA. *He rushes off.*

MATT. Ah, crap!

VAN HELSING. Before Mrs Westenra came in.

MATT (*wings*). I can't find the dress!

VAN HELSING. Forget the dress, you're a shadow.

MRS WESTENRA enters without a dress on.

Not only did she collect up all the garlic…

MRS WESTENRA. Let's get rid of this stinking stuff. And get some fresh air in here.

VAN HELSING. But the useless old bat opened the window.

She exits with window.

And there it was. His chance. Quite literally, an open window.

DRACULA approaches the screen and steps onto the truck supporting it. His shadow again creates the classic Nosferatu profile, except this time his head is visible above the screen.

He glided into the room.

He is wheeled off into stage-right wings by VAN HELSING.

And then he *flew* towards the bed.

VAN HELSING pulls on a screen double. It has a painted black shadow, identical in size and posture to what we have just seen. Sticking above it is a 2D profile photo of DRACULA's head.

VAN HELSING exits. DAN (holding screen of himself from upstage) moves towards the bed. LUCY wakes up and sees shadow-DRACULA looming over her. She offers him her neck. The bite is as sexual as it can be with the prop. VAN HELSING bursts in.

No!!

DAN exits with screen. HOLMWOOD wakes.

HOLMWOOD. Huh? Lucy!?

VAN HELSING. You fell asleep, you poopemnink! Where's the garlic? Why is the window open? Where is the window?

AL. I'll get it.

VAN HELSING. No, stay lying down! (*Mimes looking through a window.*) There he is! After him!

VAN HELSING *and* HOLMWOOD *exit through stage-left door.*

Scene Fifteen

DRACULA *enters, clipping himself on to a rope that descends from the pros.* AL *appears on the other end of rope to pull up the slack as* DRACULA *climbs onto the bed* (*the wardrobe on its back*).

VAN HELSING *and* HOLMWOOD *enter.*

VAN HELSING. He's shape-shifting! He's turning into a bat! He's going to fly away.

DRACULA *leaps. The stage-right section of the pros part collapses. Dust and rubble fall to the stage.*

Ignore it! Carry on.

AL. I'm not sure that's wise, Professor. This theatre doesn't look very safe.

VAN HELSING. Then make it safe.

AL. Let's get the pros secured. Take the rope to the back wall. Get me a ladder.

MATT *brings ladder and climbs up to tie off the broken pros.* VAN HELSING *takes the securing rope to the back wall and hooks it round a cleat.*

And we're going to need some kind of anchor. (*To audience member.*) You, sir, on your feet please. What's your name?

AL *hands the audience member the end of the rope that leads to back wall cleat and then up to the pros.*

Hold this securely, Gary [*name of audience member*]. Okay, we're ready to continue, Professor.

Sound and lighting return us to performing state.

VAN HELSING. He's shape shifting into a bat. Get on the wardrobe and fly!

DAN attempts to get on bed but is in pain from his previous jump. The stage-left section of pros falls.

AL (*to audience member*). Pull on the rope!

Audience member pulls on the rope (with AL), ripping away a section of the back wall.

What have you done, you idiot?

VAN HELSING. Look what you've done to the theatre!

Sound effect: more creaking. Stage-left pros upright falls towards the audience. AL manages to get to it.

AL. Find something to support this!

MATT (*points towards hole*). There might be something back there.

AL (*to audience member*). Gary, come and help me. (*Sotto.*) And make it look heavy.

DAN looks into the hole created in the back wall.

DAN. Bloody hell! There's a set in storage back here for what looks like a touring production of Bram Stoker's *Dracula*.

VAN HELSING. What?! A touring production of *Dracula*?! If I could get my hands on those idiots!

DAN hands him a poster.

They should be shot! The lot of them!

AL. Professor, watch out!

The last bit of pros (stage-right upright) falls onto the stage and knocks out VAN HELSING. MATT rushes over to him.

MATT. Is he all right?

AL. Well, he's not getting up.

DAN. Are you saying he's dead?

MATT. No, he's still breathing. Ladies and gentlemen, for obvious reasons, I'm afraid that we're going to have to call for an unscheduled interruption.

Please don't be alarmed, order will be restored. Please leave the theatre in an orderly fashion. There will be an announcement to let you know when you can come back in.

AL. Looking at this I'd say in about... twenty minutes. (*To audience member.*) Right, you – you're coming with us to explain your actions to the theatre management.

DAN *has wedged a broom to 'hold up' the stage-left pros. Curtains close and they exit with the audience member and dragging* VAN HELSING *off.*

Interval.

ACT TWO

Scene One

AL *and* DAN *enter, front cloth.*

AL. Ladies and gentlemen, we have good news.

DAN. And some even better news.

AL. The good news is that order has been restored, the theatre is now safe and we will be continuing.

DAN. And the even better news is that our production has been upgraded. With the loan of a set. That we found.

AL. Which I'm sure it's fine that we borrow.

DAN. Under the circumstances.

MATT *appears through the curtains.*

MATT. He's still not looking good, I think we should call an ambulance.

AL. He'll be all right.

MATT. He doesn't look all right.

DAN. He looked fine.

MATT. He looks dead.

AL. Professor Van Helsing is currently 'resting' and therefore an understudy has stepped into his shoes.

DAN. And his trousers.

MATT. No, they didn't fit him.

AL. A man whom we have *every* confidence in.

MATT. Every confidence? He's going to be…

AL. Shhhh…

MATT.…it.

AL. Exeter, we continue with: *Dracula: The Bloody Truth…*

DAN. Continued.

Music. Curtains open. Audience member (GARY) *is stood in a spotlight centre stage, wearing* VAN HELSING's *overcoat and top hat, holding a script, in front of new set. The set consists of three painted flats (on wheels). The centre one has a large gothic window (cut out). To its stage right is a painted door, ajar. On stage left is a burning fire and mantelpiece, painted on to a real door that opens in the flat.*

MATT (*sotto*). Say your line now, Gary.

GARY (*reading from a script*). Damn, we're too late, Holmwood! He's shape-shifted into a bat! We must return immediately to Miss Westenra. Look, there she is.

MATT. Not yet! We've got to get to her house first! Just walk and I'll follow you.

They walk. LUCY *wheels on a bed (a cart) and lies on it.*

Now.

GARY. Look, there she is. Oh God, we're too late. She's dead.

HOLMWOOD. No, Lucy, my love. Lucy!

GARY. It's all my fault. Pass me that fork.

HOLMWOOD *passes him a fork.*

MATT. Go on then. What does the stage direction on the next page say?

GARY. In frustration, Van Helsing stabs himself with a fork.

VAN HELSING *enters in his underwear with a bandage round his head.*

VAN HELSING. What's going on? (*To* GARY.) Who are you? Are you wearing my clothes?

AL. Listen, Professor, you were out for the count. We decided to continue because we believe in this show.

VAN HELSING. It's not a show, it's a public-information seminar! And I'm fine to carry on.

MATT. Are you sure?

VAN HELSING. You dare to question Professor Ham Velsing?

MATT. Van Helsing.

VAN HELSING. That's what I said. Vell Hancing. Hell Dancing. Just give me my clothes. And what the hell is this monstrosity?

DAN. It's the set we found back there, Professor.

VAN HELSING. A set!? You know how I feel about theatre!

DAN. I really think it's going add to the audience's enjoyment.

VAN HELSING. They're not here to enjoy themselves.

DAN. I mean, their understanding.

VAN HELSING. Fine. Let's just continue. Where are we?

MATT. Lucy's dead.

    MATT *shoves* AL *back down and exits*.

VAN HELSING. Have I stabbed myself with a fork yet?

MATT (*handing him the fork*). Not yet.

    VAN HELSING *stabs himself in the leg*.

VAN HELSING. Arghh! (*To* GARY.) Why are you still here?

DAN. You'd better come with me, Gary. It's getting serious.

    DAN *takes* GARY *back to his seat and sets furniture for next scene*.

Scene Two

VAN HELSING. I'm now going to transport you two months later. To Dr Seward's asylum in Essex… You know – Dr Seward – one of Lucy's suitors, in care of a patient called Renfield? Yes? Continue.

He limps off. SEWARD *enters and sits at desk* (*the cart*) *to write. He watches a fly buzzing. It lands on a bell, which he hits.* MARGARET *enters.*

MARGARET. You called, Dr Seward?

SEWARD. I was just swatting a fly actually, Margaret. But since you're here, has the patient been brought up?

MARGARET. Yes. Shall I show him in?

SEWARD. Take a note first, please. The subject, Renfield has been showing some interesting tendencies of late –

MARGARET (*taking notes*). Tendencies of late.

SEWARD. He insists that everyone around him is losing their minds –

MARGARET. Losing their minds.

SEWARD. But that he himself –

MARGARET. Is perfectly sane.

SEWARD (*inadvertently mimics* MARGARET*'s Scottish accent*). Is perfectly sane.

They share a look.

He's obsessed with someone he calls 'The Master'. Show him in, please.

SEWARD *moves to the birdcage.*

And how are we this morning, Mr Cornelius?

MARGARET *opens the door.*

MARGARET. In you come, Mr Renfield. Will that be all, Doctor?

RENFIELD. Yes, thank you, Margaret.

SEWARD. Thank you, Margaret. You may go.

MARGARET exits. RENFIELD sits behind SEWARD's
desk.

RENFIELD. Take a seat please, Seward.

SEWARD (*stays standing*). And how are we feeling this
morning, Renfield?

RENFIELD. Well, I'm fine. But you seem to be under the
impression that you're *my* doctor.

RENFIELD rings bell. MARGARET *enters. He approaches
her.*

Margaret, take a note – the patient's condition has worsened
since my last visit.

SEWARD (*back behind his desk*). Margaret, please note that
the patient is now under the impression that I'm under
the impression that I'm his doctor. Now tell me about
your mother.

MARGARET. My mother?

RENFIELD. Margaret, take a note. The patient is now
interested in your mother.

SEWARD. No, it's your mother I'm interested in, Renfield.

RENFIELD. Well, I'll hook you up, you old dog. She's single
and ready to mingle ever since Papa 'buried himself' in the
garden.

Sound effect: buzzing fly. RENFIELD *plucks it out of the air
and eats it.*

SEWARD. Renfield, did you just eat a fly?

RENFIELD. Eat a fly?

SEWARD. Yes, you just grabbed a fly out of the air and stuffed
it in your mouth.

RENFIELD. Don't be ridiculous. Margaret, we'll need to
increase his medication.

RENFIELD *snatches something from the desk*.

SEWARD. What was that?

RENFIELD. What?

SEWARD. You just ate a spider?

RENFIELD. What spider?

SEWARD. The spider that was on the table next to Margaret.

RENFIELD. Are you trying to suggest I ate the spider that sat down beside her?

SEWARD. Yes I am.

RENFIELD. Margaret, he thinks you're Miss Muffet.

SEWARD. Now you're just being silly. I'm here to help you. Apparently you've been writing letters to someone called 'The Master'. I've got some of them here.

Bends down to pick up a file from a desk drawer. RENFIELD *grabs the bird out of a cage and eats it*.

Renfield! Did you just eat Cornelius?

RENFIELD. What canary? The cage is empty.

SEWARD. Exactly. Because you've just eaten the contents.

RENFIELD. Contents? I thought his name was Cornelius.

SEWARD. You've even got a feather in your mouth.

RENFIELD (*takes feather out of his mouth*). What feather?

SEWARD. That feather in your hand.

RENFIELD (*drops feather to the floor*). There's no feather in my hand.

SEWARD. You just dropped it on the floor.

RENFIELD (*standing on it*). There's no feather on the floor.

SEWARD. You're standing on it. For God's sake, man! Admit it. You've eaten a fly, a spider, my bird! Whatever next?

Sound effect: cat meow. All look at the sleeping cat.

SEWARD. No! Step away from Mr Socrates, Renfield. Step away!

RENFIELD dives on the cat. SEWARD tackles him.

Margaret, get the sedative!

MARGARET injects RENFIELD in the arse.

You're going back to your cell.

They all exit.

RENFIELD (*off*). No! I must eat the cat that ate the bird, who ate the spider who ate the fly!! I don't know why I ate the fly! Perhaps I'll die! The Master! He's near! He's coming.

VAN HELSING. 'The Master?' What did he mean by that? Who was he talking about? If only I'd known back then what I know now.

Knock at the door. DRACULA enters.

DRACULA. Hello?

He wanders to the window upstage centre. MARGARET enters.

MARGARET. Excuse me. Who are you? How did you get in here?

DRACULA. I thought I might pay Dr Seward a visit. I've just moved in to Carfax Abbey, just across the way there.

MARGARET. Well, I'm afraid the doctor's rather tied up at the moment.

DRACULA. Then perhaps you can tell me if you have a... Mr Renfield residing here at the asylum. He's an old friend of mine.

MARGARET. We do. But I'm afraid that today is not a good day for visitors.

DRACULA. That's all I needed to know. Thank you, Margaret. It's been a pleasure.

He exits.

MARGARET. How did he know my name? Goodness, I feel rather faint. I think I need to sit down.

SEWARD *enters*.

SEWARD. Well, that's old Renfield sorted. Are you all right, Margaret? You've gone white.

MARGARET. The new owner of Carfax Abbey just came to see you. There was something very strange about him.

SEWARD. We're all a bit odd around here, Margaret. Even you!

MARGARET. Oh, and I almost forgot. This telegram arrived.

Curtains close behind SEWARD. *He reads telegram, pacing, but stops each time on 'STOP'.*

VAN HELSING. My dear friend Seward, STOP. Please meet me at Highgate Cemetery tonight, STOP. Will explain all when you arrive, STOP. And bring a crowbar, STOP.

SEWARD. Margaret. I'm going to London.

Scene Three

VAN HELSING. Meanwhile, Jonathan Harker has managed to escape from Dracula's castle in Transylvania. Well – his body might have made it back to London. But terrifyingly, not his mind!

Curtains open to reveal HARKER *asleep in bed. Sound effects of the* VAMPIRE BRIDES *moaning*.

HARKER. No. No, keep away from me, you harlots. Don't touch me there! No, not like that! Please, stop. Oh God, you're so beautiful. No, no. I can't! I won't let you. Stop. Stop!!! Arrgghh!

MINA *enters*.

MINA. Jonathan. Jonathan, wake up.

HARKER. Get away from me, you jezebel.

MINA. It's me – Mina. You're back at home now.

He wakes.

HARKER. Mina! Oh, my love, I'm so sorry.

MINA. What's happening to you?

HARKER. I don't know.

MINA *accidentally takes his next line and they get in a muddle.*

MINA. What was I saying?

HARKER. You were having another nightmare. We have to talk about what happened to you in Transylvania.

MINA. No. I can't face it.

HARKER. For goodness' sake, Jonathan, I'm your wife now. You must.

MINA. Yes, and I appreciate that, Mina.

HARKER. First my best friend Lucy dies and now you return in this state. (*Saving them.*) You've written down some of the things I've been saying.

MINA. Yes I have. I've written down some of the things you've been saying.

HARKER. No. They must be destroyed!

He snatches the paper and tears it up. He watches MINA *start to exit and then she stops. Pause.*

Wait! Fine, I admit it. I have a problem.

Sound effect: the BRIDES.

They're calling me again.

MINA. Who are?

HARKER. Them. He had me under a spell.

MINA. Who did?

HARKER. I can't even say his name.

MINA. You mean Count…

HARKER. Don't say it!

MINA. Dracula.

HARKER. Yes.

MINA. What did he do to you, Jonathan? I have to know.

She picks up HARKER*'s diary.*

Maybe this will explain things.

HARKER. No! I forbid you from reading my diary.

HARKER *snatches the diary and tries to set fire to it.* MINA *takes it from him.*

MINA. Stop it, Jonathan! If you won't talk to me then you need to talk to someone else. And I'm going to lock this away in our safety deposit box until you're ready to face what happened to you.

HARKER. Fine. But don't read it!

MINA. I'm not going to! And I'm locking poor Lucy's diary away too. I won't be long.

HARKER. He's close. He's here in London. I can feel it!

MINA *exits. Sound effect: the* BRIDES. *Curtains close.*

Scene Four

Sound effect: wind, rain and Big Ben chiming. Front cloth –
MINA *crosses, battling with an umbrella and ends up dropping*
the diary. The curtains part. DRACULA *steps out.*

DRACULA. You dropped your book. Allow me.

He pings her umbrella open.

It would be a shame for this to get wet. It looks important.

MINA. Yes.

DRACULA. J–H. Your diary?

MINA. My husband's actually.

DRACULA (*handing it back*). Interesting.

MINA. Thank you. (*Sneezes.*) And now I've forgotten my
handkerchief. I'm just having such a terrible day.

DRACULA *whips out a handkerchief.*

DRACULA. Here.

MINA. You're so kind. I'd forget my head if it wasn't attached
to my neck.

DRACULA. An interesting idea.

VAN HELSING (*appearing*). Look – he's so weird. But she
suspects nothing. Instead she says…

MINA. It's rare to meet someone who takes time to help
strangers in this crazy city.

DRACULA. Well, I'm something of a stranger myself here in
London.

MINA. Oh?

DRACULA. Although I have just taken up membership of a
club around the corner. Let me buy you a drink. It'll give you
a chance to dry out until this storm passes.

MINA. Um…

DRACULA. I'm thinking of buying some property in the city
and would really appreciate some advice on suitable locations.

MINA. Thank you, but I don't think so.

DRACULA. I understand. Goodbye then.

He walks away.

MINA. I suppose a quick cup of tea wouldn't hurt.

DRACULA. Exactly, it won't hurt at all. And neither would a cocktail.

MINA. A cocktail?

DRACULA. Whatever you prefer. It's just along here.

They exit. VAN HELSING *appears at pros door.*

VAN HELSING. You see what he's like!? A master of manipulation and deception. Such grace and evil juxtaposed within one being. This is what we're up against, people.

Scene Five

HARKER *enters.*

HARKER. Mina, where are you?

MINA *enters.*

MINA. Jonathan?

HARKER. Mina, thank God.

MINA. What on earth are you doing running around London in your dressing gown?

HARKER. Looking for you. You said you were coming straight home.

MINA. For goodness' sake, I just stopped off for a cocktail.

HARKER. A cocktail?

MINA. Yes.

HARKER. In the middle of the day?

MINA. Yes.

HARKER. Why would you do that?

MINA (*confused*). I don't know. (*Beat*.) My umbrella broke and…

HARKER. So you went for a cocktail?

MINA. Okay, I appreciate it sounds a bit odd. But it wasn't my idea.

HARKER. What do you mean?

MINA. There was a man.

HARKER. –

MINA. It wasn't like that!

HARKER. It sounds exactly like that. Maybe it was… him.

MINA. Do you mean Count –

HARKER. Don't say it –

MINA. Dracula. Jonathan, you're obsessed.

HARKER. Describe him! What was he like?

MINA. Please. People are watching.

HARKER. Let them watch, this is important, damn it!

MINA. You're completely overacting. Reacting. You're obsessed that danger is lurking around every corner.

PAPERBOY (*off*). Extra, extra, read all about it… Bloofer Lady of Highgate strikes again.

HARKER *has magically acquired a newspaper* (*through flap in curtain*).

HARKER. You see!

MINA. What's a Bloofer Lady?

HARKER. I've no idea. But it doesn't sound good.

SEWARD *approaches*.

SEWARD. Mina?

MINA. Dr Seward. Jonathan, this is Dr Seward.

HARKER. And?

MINA. Lucy's friend who I was telling you about.

SEWARD. Good day, sir.

> HARKER *is clearly agitated*.

> Is everything quite all right, old chap?

MINA. So what brings you to the city, Doctor?

SEWARD. The professor sent me a rather cryptic telegram asking me to meet him at Highgate Cemetery tonight with a crowbar.

MINA. Bit random.

SEWARD. I know, right?

HARKER. He's close. He's here.

MINA (*upset*). He's not well. He needs psychiatric help!

SEWARD. Listen, why don't the two of you come out to my asylum in the country on the weekend. See it as a chance to get away from it all for a while. (*Private*.) I'll examine him then.

MINA. We'd love to. Thank you.

HARKER (*off*). Line up and explain yourselves to me!

MINA. Jonathan, leave those pigeons alone. Goodbye, Doctor. Have a nice evening at the cemetery.

> MINA *exits*.

SEWARD. Until the weekend.

> *Curtains open fully to reveal the cemetery.*

Scene Six

The screens have spun and have spooky trees painted on the back.

SEWARD. Professor?

VAN HELSING (*off*). Shut up.

SEWARD. Where are you?

VAN HELSING (*off*). Shut up.

> VAN HELSING *approaches behind him.*

> Don't move.

SEWARD. Jesus! What's all this about?

VAN HELSING. You're about to find out.

HOLMWOOD (*off*). Professor?

VAN HELSING. Shut up.

HOLMWOOD (*off*). Where are you?

VAN HELSING. Shut up.

> HOLMWOOD *enters.*

SEWARD. Arthur.

HOLMWOOD. Dr Seward.

VAN HELSING. Will you both keep your voices down! Now tell me, gentlemen, what do you know of the Bloofer Lady?

SEWARD. Only what I've just read in the papers. Some kind of creature that's been biting the necks of children.

HOLMWOOD. Just another sensationalist headline, no doubt.

VAN HELSING. Is it!?

HOLMWOOD. I don't know.

VAN HELSING. Follow me.

HOLMWOOD. Into the crypt where Lucy's laid to rest!?

SEWARD. Professor, if Scotland Yard were to discover us loitering about the cemetery at this hour, there's a good chance we'll end up in the cells.

VAN HELSING. Better that than dead.

He exits. They share a look.

(*Off.*) Come on!

They follow.

(*Off.*) Look! See how the padlock has been ripped off the gate!

Sound effect: opening of an iron gate.

This way.

They enter on to stage (the crypt) through the new hole in the back wall. The cupboard is on its side (to represent coffin) with a stone lid.

Crowbar, Seward. I'm going to prove something to you.

HOLMWOOD. By opening Lucy's coffin! You're insane.

VAN HELSING. Am I!?

HOLMWOOD. I don't know.

VAN HELSING *and* SEWARD *lever up the stone lid.*

VAN HELSING. There. What do you see? Look!

HOLMWOOD. Where's my dead fiancée?

VAN HELSING. I think we're about to find out.

The stone lid that SEWARD *has levered up comes down, squishing* HOLMWOOD's *head. It is then lifted off by* VAN HELSING *and* SEWARD *on to his foot.*

Outside, now!

The three exit. LUCY *appears.* VAN HELSING, HOLMWOOD *and* SEWARD *enter.*

Get down!

They cower behind a bush.

SEWARD. The Bloofer Lady?

She turns.

HOLMWOOD. Lucy!

VAN HELSING. Get down, man!

SEWARD. It can't be! I signed her death certificate.

LUCY. Arthur, come to me.

VAN HELSING. Do NOT respond to her.

HOLMWOOD. Yes, Lucy, it's me!

VAN HELSING. No! That is not Lucy!

HOLMWOOD. Are you saying I don't know my own fiancée!?

VAN HELSING. Your fiancée is dead! That creature has taken
over her body.

LUCY. Kiss me, Arthur.

She walks towards them. VAN HELSING *holds up
a crucifix.*

VAN HELSING. Stay away from us!

SEWARD. Be gone, you foul creature!

SEWARD *throws tufts of earth at her, then the bush.*

LUCY. Arthur, come to me.

HOLMWOOD (*running to her*). Lucy!

VAN HELSING. Arthur, no!

LUCY *is about to bite* HOLMWOOD's *neck.* SEWARD *runs
forward and clangs her with a spade.*

HOLMWOOD (*to* SEWARD). How dare you!

He snatches the spade and clangs SEWARD.

SEWARD. I'm trying to save you, you fool!

SEWARD *takes spade and swipes. But* HOLMWOOD *ducks
and he clangs* VAN HELSING, *who takes the spade and
clangs them both.*

VAN HELSING. Enough with the spades!

SEWARD. Where's she gone?

VAN HELSING. The sun is about to rise. She will have taken refuge back in her coffin.

They exit. LUCY *enters the crypt and attempts to elegantly clamber up on to the coffin. Then lies, face up. The men enter.*

SEWARD. What happens now, Professor?

VAN HELSING. Someone will have to hammer a stake through her heart and cut off her head.

SEWARD. Someone?

VAN HELSING. It must be the person closest to her.

They look at HOLMWOOD. VAN HELSING *passes him a stake.*

HOLMWOOD. No! No!

VAN HELSING. Do you want her to walk the earth in a state of unholy unrest for the rest of eternity?

HOLMWOOD. I won't do it.

VAN HELSING. This isn't just to save her. This is to release her victims – the innocent children she's preyed upon.

SEWARD (*grabbing* HOLMWOOD). For God's sake, Arthur. Just drive the damn stake through her heart.

VAN HELSING *hands* HOLMWOOD *a rock.*

VAN HELSING. Do it!

HOLMWOOD *climbs up, straddles* LUCY *and drives a stake through her heart, then gets down, distraught.* VAN HELSING *produces a piece of slate.*

Now remove her head!

HOLMWOOD. No!

VAN HELSING. Do it!

SEWARD. For God's sake, Arthur. Cut her noggin off!

SEWARD *slaps him. Then* VAN HELSING *does, then* SEWARD *punches him in the stomach.*

HOLMWOOD *takes the slate.* VAN HELSING *and* SEWARD *turn* LUCY *on to her front. The end of the stake protrudes through her back.* HOLMWOOD *straddles her with the slate.*

VAN HELSING. Take these signs and in the name of the Lord they shall cast out devils. They shall speak with new tongues and the body will be recovered ever to rest in peace.

SEWARD *holds* LUCY*'s head.* HOLMWOOD *brings the slate down on her neck. Her head departs.* SEWARD *tosses the head into the audience.*

SEWARD. Be gone!!

VAN HELSING. No! Bring her head back. Her mouth must be stuffed with garlic.

SEWARD *has to collect the head from the audience.* HOLMWOOD *is very distressed.*

It's vital that we finish the job properly.

VAN HELSING *stuffs garlic into the dummy head's mouth.* SEWARD *comforts* HOLMWOOD.

SEWARD. Chin up. You'll meet someone else, mate.

VAN HELSING *places* LUCY*'s head back on her shoulders.*

VAN HELSING. Gentlemen, we can now leave her to rest in peace.

HOLMWOOD (*still straddling* LUCY) *takes the head and starts to kiss it.* VAN HELSING *takes it from him* (*each time*) *and replaces it.*

No! Arthur, you've done an amazing thing but this isn't over yet. Put the head down. We must now track down her master and kill him. Put the head down!

SEWARD. For God's sake, man, get a grip of yourself.

He pulls HOLMWOOD *off* LUCY.

VAN HELSING. We'll need an operations venue.

SEWARD. My asylum?

VAN HELSING. Perfect. To the asylum! Leave the head!

They exit. Blackout. After a few moments the lights come up.
VAN HELSING *and* SEWARD *are repositioning the flats
but* AL*'s head is stuck in the trick hole for the head-cutting
illusion.*

Not yet!

Blackout. Lights up again. VAN HELSING *and* SEWARD
are helping AL *pull his head out.*

Blackout. Lights back up and AL *sets the table, then
attempts to exit through the painted door.*

VAN HELSING *and* SEWARD *are carrying wardrobe/
coffin off.*

That's a painted door. Use the fire door.

AL *opens the door in the flat that has a fire painted on to it.
He reveals* MATT *changing – down to his underwear,
inadvertently mooning the audience.*

Go around!

AL *exits.*

Scene Seven

SEWARD *and* VAN HELSING *enter from wings*.

SEWARD. Welcome to my asylum, Professor. So, what are your thoughts?

VAN HELSING. We should wait for Mina and her husband to arrive. If we are to track down this monster we will need our collective minds.

Sound effect: doorbell.

SEWARD. Sounds like them now.

MATT (*off*). Not yet!

   VAN HELSING *and* SEWARD *fill*.

VAN HELSING. So, this is your office in the asylum where you work?

   VAN HELSING *hangs his coat up on a painted hook but it falls to the floor.*

SEWARD. Yes. It's a work in progress.

VAN HELSING (*putting coat back on*). Bit chilly actually.

SEWARD. I'll stick another log on the fire.

   He picks up a log and throws it at the fire. It bounces off the flat. He pushes it into the flat so it sticks out.

   Whisky?

   He attempts to pick up a painted bottle on a painted mantelpiece. MINA *and* HARKER *enter.*

   Mina. Jonathan. Welcome.

MINA. Hello, Doctor. Professor, this is my husband, Jonathan Harker.

VAN HELSING. Pleased to meet you, Mr…?

   HARKER *has distractedly turned away.*

MINA. Shall we get started?

SEWARD. Just before we do, Lucy, I have some rather upsetting news. It's about poor Mina.

MINA. Other way around.

He realises his mistake and backs up for another go.

SEWARD. Just before we do, Mina, I have some rather upsetting news. It's about poor Lucy. Let me explain.

Dramatic music. SEWARD *mimes scene retelling the killing of* LUCY. *Music ends.*

MINA. 'Kin hell! So Lucy was the Bloofer Lady?

VAN HELSING. I'm afraid so.

HARKER. Just like the vampire brides.

They all stare at him.

No! I can't talk of it.

VAN HELSING. What vampire brides?

MINA. Jonathan had a terrible experience whilst working in Transylvania.

VAN HELSING. Transylvania? Mr Harker, if we are going to get to the bottom of this vile business, I must know everything that happened to you there

HARKER. I've told you! I can't talk about it.

MINA. But he *did* keep a record of the experience in his diary.

VAN HELSING. It's imperative I see that diary. Where is it?

HARKER. Don't tell him!

MINA. It's in our safety deposit box in London, along with Lucy's diary.

VAN HELSING. We need those diaries!

MINA. Then I must return to London.

SEWARD (*opening door*). I shall accompany you, Mrs Harker.

MINA. Thank you, Doctor. I'm sure the two of you will find plenty to talk about.

They exit. Dramatic music. HARKER *and* VAN HELSING *stand looking very awkward. The music builds to a climax.* SEWARD *and* MINA *re-enter.*

MINA. We made good time. (*Hands over the diaries*.) Here.

VAN HELSING. I'll need everyone else's too.

The remaining diaries are produced.

Right. Let's piece this mother together.

Montage with music. Mime surprises, laughs, horror, realisations – until music cuts.

Smoking windmills, I think I've got it. Gentlemen… and lady. I believe that the man Jonathan went to see in Transylvania is the same man that travelled to Whitby with fifty boxes of earth and killed Lucy. The same man that took Mina for a cocktail in London. The same man who has bought Carfax Abbey next door. The same man who Renfield has been rambling about. And that man, is Count –

Sound effect: dramatic stab.

Dracula!

Sound effect: four more stabs.

ALL. 'Kin hell.

MINA. Jonathan, I'm so sorry for not believing you.

HARKER. It's okay, Mina. It's just such a relief to finally get it all off my chest. (*Starts crying*.) I feel like a new man.

VAN HELSING. There's no time for tears, Mr Harker. Count Dracula's daytime refuge is his boxes of earth – all shipped next door to Carfax Abbey. Gentlemen, do you understand what we must do?

SEWARD. Yes!

VAN HELSING. Do you!?

VAN HELSING walks towards him. Intense dramatic sound effects which stop when he reaches him.

SEWARD. No.

VAN HELSING. We must destroy those boxes tonight. Mina, I think it's wise that you stay here. That's not me being sexist, I just feel that…well… as I say, I'm not sexist but…

MINA. It's fine, Professor. I understand.

HARKER. Do you?

> HARKER *walks towards her. Intense dramatic sound effects, which stops when he reaches her.*

MINA. Not entirely, no.

VAN HELSING. And I can appreciate that. Gentlemen, follow me!

MINA. Be careful, Jonathan.

HARKER. I will, Mina. Stay safe.

> *He kisses her on lips and exits.*

SEWARD. Stay safe.

> *He kisses her on lips and exits.*

Scene Eight

MINA *is left alone, restlessly pacing* SEWARD's *office. She sits at the table. She leafs through a diary.*

MINA. Perhaps –

> *Blackout. Then lights come back up.*

Perhaps there's something we've missed. Some clue or other. Surely we don't yet have the complete picture. Renfield – what was it Dr Seward was saying about him? He called Count Dracula, 'The Master'. How does he serve him? I can't sit around here waiting. I have to find out.

> *She exits then makes a downstage cross while the set flats are moved behind her.* DRACULA *sets a dummy of* RENFIELD *and bites it. He then retreats into shadows.* MINA *peers into* RENFIELD's *cell through hatch in the door in the back wall.*

Mr Renfield? Can I have a word? Mr Renfield!?

The door swings open.

Open?

She enters. She rolls the dummy body over.

Dead?

DRACULA. Good evening, Mrs Harker. How lovely to see you again.

He closes the door.

MINA. No.

DRACULA. All alone? Well, not completely, of course. But I don't imagine you're getting much conversation out of old Renfield.

MINA. Get away from me. Stay back.

DRACULA. I'm not going to hurt you. Your photograph doesn't do you justice, you know.

MINA. What do you want?

DRACULA. When the cat's away, the mice can play.

MINA. I'm not frightened of you.

DRACULA. Oh, come on, Mina, you're better than that. Of course you're frightened. But I'm here to change all that. The world can be so... unpleasant at times. There should be more love in it, don't you agree?

He raises his hand towards her neck.

Such a beautiful neck.

He moves in. She suddenly grips his wrist.

MINA. No!

DRACULA. Trust me. We have an inseparable bond, you and I. A bond that will travel with us into eternity.

He bites her neck. She accepts. DRACULA *opens his shirt and cuts his chest with a knife,* MINA *sucks his blood.*

I am yours for ever!

HARKER *and* VAN HELSING (*brandishing a crucifix*) *enter.*

VAN HELSING. Get away from her! Surrender yourself to me!

HARKER. Mina!

DRACULA *throws them both to the floor with a raised hand.*

DRACULA. Surrender? To you? You have no idea what you're dealing with, do you, you silly little man?

HARKER (*approaching*). Mina.

DRACULA. Hello again, Mr Harker. How are the sexy dreams?

Oh, your wife tasted good. Exceptional, I'd say.

HARKER. Why, you –

DRACULA *raises his hand. Blackout. When lights come up,* DRACULA (*and* RENFIELD*'s dummy body*) *are gone.*

VAN HELSING. No!

HARKER. Where did he go?

VAN HELSING. He shape-shifted.

HARKER. Shape-shifted?

VAN HELSING. He turned into a bat. Don't try to make sense of it. It's too fooking weird.

HARKER. Mina, my love, I should never have left you alone. This is all my fault.

VAN HELSING. There's no time for tears. Pull yourself together, man.

MINA. What's happening to me? I feel so peculiar.

VAN HELSING. You're becoming a vampire. And the only way to save you is to destroy Count Dracula!

HARKER. How?

VAN HELSING. By hunting him. Until he turns to bay, like an exhausted stag. Tonight we destroyed all but four of his boxes. We must find those remaining ones.

HOLMWOOD. Where do we even begin, Professor?

VAN HELSING. Not where. How.

MINA. By hypnotising me.

VAN HELSING. Exactly. A bond has now been established between the two of them. Mina herself is our best hope of saving... Mina herself. Where's Dr Seward?

SEWARD *enters*.

SEWARD. Here.

VAN HELSING. Get me a chair. And dim the lights.

SEWARD *sets chair for* MINA, *downstage right*.

Mina, I need you to trust me. All I need you to do is to follow the light of this candle.

He produces a trick candle and lights it.

Focus on the flame. Relax. Connect with his mind. When the flame is extinguished you will see what he sees.

He blows out the flame and the candle disappears.

Mina, tell me what you see.

MINA. Yes, Master. Yes, Master. I will obey you, Master!

Tension builds, everyone leans in. Suddenly MINA *lunges, screaming, towards* VAN HELSING's *neck*.

HARKER. Mina!

They get her back onto the chair. She calms.

VAN HELSING. You must control the urge. Now think! What can you see?

Scene Nine

MINA. I can see… London.

SEWARD and HOLMWOOD exit. Curtains close.
VAN HELSING exits through stage-right door.

A street with a park. A tall house. A blue front door.

HARKER. This way, Professor!

Curtains open halfway to reveal a coffin.

SEWARD. In here!

VAN HELSING. Stand back! With this holy water I banish the evil from this earth!

HARKER. One down. Three to go.

VAN HELSING steps downstage back to MINA. Curtains close.

VAN HELSING. Mina. What else are you seeing?

MINA. A cobbled street. A stone stairway leading down.

VAN HELSING. I need more!

MINA. A wooden door.

SEWARD (*pulls curtain onstage stage left*). Is this it?

HARKER (*pulls curtain onstage stage right*). No! (*Then runs into wings.*)

VAN HELSING. What do you hear, Mina?

Sound effect: dogs barking.

MINA. Dogs. Many dogs.

SEWARD (*off*). Mile End dog pound is two streets from here!

Curtains open from each side to create two columns.

HARKER (*enters through the back-wall door*). This is it! Look, another box!

He lifts up 2D coffin. SEWARD enters through stage-left door. VAN HELSING pours holy water on it and destroys coffin two.

VAN HELSING. Next!

MINA. Brick walls. Steel. Cranes.

VAN HELSING. What do you smell?

MINA. Fish. I hear clattering of chains. Men shouting.

HARKER. The docks!

They run on the spot.

MINA. A steel door. An empty warehouse.

They turn and face three empty spaces created by curtain columns. They criss-cross the stage.

SEWARD. Which one? There are doors everywhere.

VAN HELSING. Focus, Mina.

MINA. Fleur.

VAN HELSING. Fleur? What does that mean?

HARKER. Flower in French.

VAN HELSING. So we're looking for flowers?

SEWARD. No! Look, Professor. The name of that ship – (*Pointing to audience.*) *Le Petit Fleur.*

HARKER. It must be in that warehouse next to where it's docked.

VAN HELSING. Come on!

They run. Curtains open fully.

SEWARD. There!

SEWARD *lifts coffin three and* VAN HELSING *deals with it. He returns to* MINA. SEWARD *and* HARKER *exit.*

VAN HELSING. One more!

MINA. Sea.

VAN HELSING. See what?

MINA. Ocean. Waves.

Sound effect: ship's horn. VAN HELSING *looks out to audience.* DOCK BOY *enters.*

VAN HELSING. You there! Dock boy. That ship there!

DOCK BOY. That cargo ship?

VAN HELSING. Are there any passengers on board?

DOCK BOY. Only one. A tall thin gentleman. He wanted a box of earth transported. Paid top dollar. Insisted he had to travel with it.

VAN HELSING. Where's it headed?

DOCK BOY. Gdańsk.

DOCK BOY *exits.* SEWARD *enters.*

VAN HELSING. He must be returning to his castle to take refuge. If he reaches that sanctuary before us, he'll become more powerful than we can possibly imagine. Seward, take the next boat to Gdańsk with Harker and keep on his tail.

HARKER (*entering*). What are you going to do, Professor?

VAN HELSING. Cut him off. Mina and I will head south via Constantinople.

SEWARD. And create a classic pincer movement.

VAN HELSING. Exactly. Good luck, gentlemen.

HARKER *and* SEWARD *exit. Sound effect: the sea.*

I chartered a ship to Constantinople. But Mina was becoming less and less like herself by the hour. She was finding it very difficult to stay awake during the day.

MINA. I can't seem to stay awake during the day.

VAN HELSING. And had almost entirely lost her appetite.

MINA. I've almost entirely lost my appetite.

VAN HELSING. We were running out of time. It took us three days to reach the Borgo Pass.

Scene Ten

GYPSIES *enter on horse and trap. The horse ends up facing the wrong way.*

VAN HELSING. You there! Stop! (*To audience*.) Luckily, I speak a little Romanian. We urgently need a lift.

HELSING *and* MINA *sit on the cart.*

To Dracula's castle. As fast as possible.

WIFE. Dracula's castle!? No! Are you mad?!

VAN HELSING. I'll give you all this money.

DRIVER. Take the money. We can buy a real horse.

Sound effect: a whip crack, a horse and cart.

VAN HELSING. The journey took four hours.

Sound effect: the horse stops.

DRIVER (*pointing*). Count Dracula's castle.

VAN HELSING. But it seemed like less.

WIFE. You must take this crucifix with you.

VAN HELSING. Don't worry, lady, I've got it covered.

GYPSIES *exit with cart.*

MINA. The Master! He's coming.

VAN HELSING. Yes he is, Mina. And soon this will all be over. Deprived of his boxes of earth he'll be weak. His ability to shape-shift will be lost. He'll be no stronger than a normal man. Count Dracula is about to meet his end.

MINA *lunges towards* VAN HELSING.

No, Mina, no!

Sound effect: DRACULA *getting closer. Wolves howling,* BRIDES *moaning.*

This is it!

Enter DRACULA.

DRACULA. Step aside, Professor.

VAN HELSING. You're not going into your castle, Dracula.

> VAN HELSING *presents a crucifix.* DRACULA *uses his force to throw it aside.* MINA *lunges towards* VAN HELSING. DRACULA *steps closer. It seems all is lost.*

Get away from me!

> HARKER *enters with a three-metre-high crucifix* (*constructed out of the broken arch*).

> DRACULA *turns and the crucifix falls, crushing him. He dies a dramatic death.* MINA *is released from his spell.*

MINA. Jonathan!

HARKER. Mina! Thank God you're all right.

MINA. Professor, you've done it. He's dead.

VAN HELSING. We all did it. You, me, Jonathan, Seward? Where's Seward?

HARKER. He got delayed.

MINA. I'm so happy, I could sing!

HARKER. I'm so happy, I could listen to you sing. And I don't suppose the professor will mind, either.

VAN HELSING. That's right, Jonathan. I don't mind either.

> *Song.*

MINA.
> It's a new day,
> The sun is up above,
> And all the birds sound,
> So very full of love.
>
> It's a bright day,
> With a very blue sky,
> And I feel so gay,
> And this is the reason why.

ALL.
>   Because he's dead!
>   Dracula's dead,
>   Cos we drove a cross,
>   Right through his head,
>   He wanted us together,
>   But we'll always be apart,
>   Cos we nailed a fooking stake,
>   Right through his heart.

MINA (*spoken*). And what would've happened if we hadn't
    have killed him, Professor?

VAN HELSING.
>   You would've died,
>   Been lost for good,
>   Become a Dracula bride,
>   Oh yes indeed you would.

HARKER.
>   That would've been bad,
>   I would've beat myself up
>   I would've taken the blame,
>   And probably gone insane.

ALL.
>   But instead he's dead!
>   Dracula's dead.
>   Cos we drove a cross,
>   Right through his head,
>   He wanted us together,
>   But we'll always be apart,
>   Cos we nailed a fooking stake,
>   Right through his heart.

As audience applaud…

VAN HELSING. Shut up! Shut up! That's the ending you want,
    isn't it?! You liberal, happy-ending-loving, theatre types.
    Well, that's not what happened! I'll tell you what really
    happened.

Cart has been reset. Scene restarts.

Mina and I got to the Borgo Pass, yes. And we got a lift on the horse and trap, yes. The journey took four hours.

DRACULA (*pointing*). Welcome to my castle.

VAN HELSING. But it seemed like less.

He walks away then stops.

Wait… *YOUR* castle!?

DRIVER *reveals himself to be* DRACULA *in disguise. He stands and opens his cape fully.*

MINA. Master!

DRACULA *lowers cape to reveal the woman beside him to be a* VAMPIRE BRIDE.

DRACULA. Finally, we will be together!

VAN HELSING. No!

VAN HELSING *approaches but is thrown aside downstage centre.* MINA *walks to* DRACULA, *who lifts her into his arms.*

No!!

Curtains close, to leave VAN HELSING *in front of the cloth.*

Scene Eleven

Front cloth.

VAN HELSING. You see, life isn't like it is in the storybooks. Or like it is in Bram Stoker's ridiculous fiction. Right now and possibly for the rest of eternity, Mina Harker will be incarcerated in Count Dracula's castle in Transylvania. Destined, alongside his existing three vampire brides, to forever worship their master and crave the blood of the living. And what happened to Jonathan Harker?... I hear you ask!?

Curtains open to reveal SEWARD's *office.* SEWARD *rings bell.*

MARGARET (*entering*). Shall I show in our new patient, Dr Seward?

SEWARD. Thank you, Margaret.

She opens door.

MARGARET. Please come in, Mr Harker.

HARKER *enters.*

SEWARD. And how are you feeling this morning, Jonathan?

HARKER. I'm feeling fine, Seward. But you seem to be under the impression that you're my doctor.

HARKER *eats a fly out of the air.*

SEWARD. Jonathan, did you just eat a fly?

HARKER. Eat a fly? No.

SEWARD. Yes you did. And that spider.

HARKER. What spider?

SEWARD. You just ate a spider. No, step away from Cornelius the Second. Margaret, get the sedative. No, not Mr Socrates!

Curtains close on the chaos.

VAN HELSING. Ladies and gentlemen and your offspring, this concludes my account of the true story of Count Dracula. Yes, he is still very much alive. Take care of yourselves, and each other. For he could be... anywhere.

Massive sting. DRACULA *bursts through the curtain behind him. Reprise of song.*

ALL.
> Yeah Dracula's alive!
> Yeah he's very well,
> And he could be anywhere,
> From here to hell.
> And if you don't believe us,
> Well good luck to you.
> Just wait until he sucks your blood,
> And then you'll be a vampire too.
> Cos he's not dead!
> Yeah that's what I said.
> He could be anywhere,
> He might be under your bed,
> Or he could be in your cupboard,
> So you'd better go check,
> Or he'll sink his fooking teeth,
> Into your neck.

End.

Other Adaptations in this Series

ANIMAL FARM
Ian Wooldridge
Adapted from George Orwell

ANNA KARENINA
Helen Edmundson
Adapted from Leo Tolstoy

ARABIAN NIGHTS
Dominic Cooke

AROUND THE WORLD IN 80 DAYS
Laura Eason
Adapted from Jules Verne

THE CANTERBURY TALES
Mike Poulton
Adapted from Geoffrey Chaucer

A CHRISTMAS CAROL
Karen Louise Hebden
Adapted from Charles Dickens

CORAM BOY
Helen Edmundson
Adapted from Jamila Gavin

DAVID COPPERFIELD
Alastair Cording
Adapted from Charles Dickens

DIARY OF A NOBODY
Hugh Osborne
Adapted from George Grossmith
& Wheedon Grossmith

DR JEKYLL AND MR HYDE
David Edgar
Adapted from Robert Louis Stevenson

DRACULA
Liz Lochhead
Adapted from Bram Stoker

EMMA
Martin Millar and Doon MacKichan
Adapted from Jane Austen

FRANKENSTEIN
Patrick Sandford
Adapted from Mary Shelley

GREAT EXPECTATIONS
Nick Ormerod and Declan Donnellan
Adapted from Charles Dickens

THE HAUNTING
Hugh Janes
Adapted from Charles Dickens

HIS DARK MATERIALS
Nicholas Wright
Adapted from Philip Pullman

THE HOUND OF
THE BASKERVILLES
Steven Canny & John Nicholson
Adapted from Arthur Conan Doyle

JANE EYRE
Polly Teale
Adapted from Charlotte Brontë

JEEVES AND WOOSTER IN
PERFECT NONSENSE
The Goodale Brothers
Adapted from P.G. Wodehouse

THE JUNGLE BOOK
Stuart Paterson
Adapted from Rudyard Kipling

KENSUKE'S KINGDOM
Stuart Paterson
Adapted from Michael Morpurgo

KES
Lawrence Till
Adapted from Barry Hines

THE MASSIVE TRAGEDY
OF MADAME BOVARY
John Nicholson & Javier Marzan
Adapted from Gustave Flaubert

NOUGHTS & CROSSES
Dominic Cooke
Adapted from Malorie Blackman

THE RAGGED TROUSERED
PHILANTHROPISTS
Howard Brenton
Adapted from Robert Tressell

THE RAILWAY CHILDREN
Mike Kenny
Adapted from E. Nesbit

SWALLOWS AND AMAZONS
Helen Edmundson and Neil Hannon
Adapted from Arthur Ransome

TREASURE ISLAND
Stuart Paterson
Adapted from Robert Louis Stevenson

THE WIND IN THE WILLOWS
Mike Kenny
Adapted from Kenneth Grahame

www.nickhernbooks.co.uk

facebook.com/nickhernbooks

twitter.com/nickhernbooks